Milk

ALICE KINSELLA

Milk

On motherhood and madness

PICADOR

First published 2023 by Picador
an imprint of Pan Macmillan
The Smithson, 6 Briset Street, London ECIM 5NR
EU representative: Macmillan Publishers Ireland Ltd, 1st Floor,
The Liffey Trust Centre, 117–126 Sheriff Street Upper,
Dublin 1, DOI YC43
Associated companies throughout the world
www.panmacmillan.com

ISBN 978-1-5290-9794-8

1 3 5 7 9 8 6 4 2

A CIP catalogue record for this book is available from the British Library.

Typeset by Palimpsest Book Production Ltd, Falkirk, Stirlingshire
Printed and bound by CPI Group (UK) Ltd, Croydon, CR0 4YY

Visit **www.picador.com** to read more about all our books
and to buy them. You will also find features, author interviews and
news of any author events, and you can sign up for e-newsletters
so that you're always first to hear about our new releases.

For E and É. I love you.
And for my grandmother, Cáit, Bean Uí Néill.

Author's Note

Everything in this book is refutable.

The people that feature, namely my mother and my son, bear only the faintest resemblance to their real-life counterparts. These glimpses of representations are poor imitations of the complex individuals they are. In this book, they serve as shadows, temporary ideas to the person who was writing it at that time.

Reading it now, I find myself disagreeing with things, questioning ideas, desperate to erase what I (now) see as my past ignorance. But I, in my present state, knowing what I know now, didn't write this book. So, I leave it be.

I don't call this book fiction, as I at no point intentionally made anything up, but I would not be bold enough to claim it as fact either.

It is what it is, the at-times chaotic musings of a woman trying to write her way out of madness.

Alice Kinsella, spring 2022

−9

It starts with my breasts. Two comets about to burst apart entering the earth's atmosphere. I think, this is what it will be now, parts of my body turning into other things.

A living metaphor. Become poetry.

Window (0, +1)

My son is born during a particularly hot July. Our new eco-friendly house is designed for west coast winters. We sweat away in futuristic humidity. I become obsessed with water.

I sit by the nursery window, rocking this warm bundle to sleep. Outside, I can see trees, a mountain, the ivy-clad wall of an abandoned building. We live in town, so I am lucky to have a view like this. I'm trying to make a habit of reminding myself how lucky I am.

I can also see two streetlamps.

By day I don't notice them, but by night, when heat breaks into a vicious, urgent rain, the lamps bring water into focus. They look like light peeking through a crack of an open doorway. Two doors in the sky.

It seems to rain only at night. The summer is late in its ending, the days still hot, people still filling the beaches. But at night, rain. The water, white in the light, sprays.

Perhaps this is one of the things I'm not noticing properly.

The nursery, dimly lit and quiet, feels hermetically sealed from the world. It is too dark to see if drops are hitting the glass. The triple glazing blocks out all sound. All I can hear is the gentle pant of the baby's breathing. His breath is warm and milky. A little sour, not in a bad way, like a rich yoghurt.

Outside, through the window, I see the two white torches of furious rain. I wrap my son in a blanket and nudge the window open to the cooling splashes.

When morning comes, I forget to look for the street-lamps. There is too much to do. Changing feeding laundry pain medication bathing rocking burping repeating. It's easy to forget things.

When I look out the window by day, I see them again: mountain, the ivy, and the relentlessly blue sky of this summer that will not end. I hear the traffic cutting through town, on the way to and from the beaches that hug the bay.

The town is a baby. Lulled asleep in the cradle of the bay. The two mountains, postcard iconic. To the north, the father's table, and closer, softer, the mother. Atop the woman mountain the queen's grave is perched like a mocking nipple.

·

In the hospital they wanted me to feed faster. They had me use shields, little plastic hats for my nipples. Now the baby gets confused by the softness of my skin. His world is plastic, bottle teats and silicone, while I milk myself, a sore and heavy farm animal.

·

At night my son sleeps well. I know this because I watch him. Sleep when the baby sleeps, everyone says. *Ha.* I sit in the rocking chair in the nursery, the small weight of heat asleep in my arms. I vary, to keep myself alert, between watching my son, and watching the white of the doorways fill and empty with rain.

•

I watch my son in the bath. His shocked face is soothed by the warm water. He knows this better than the cupping of my hands or the rotating light projections on the bedroom ceiling. This is familiar to him. Not two weeks ago he was a creature of water.

•

The sound of the rain fuels the obsession. A rhythmic pelting on the windows, like a jar of pennies spilled on the floor.

When the baby is unsettled, I pat his bum and make shushing sounds. In the womb his bum was close to the beating of my heart. The shhhing lulls him like the lap of amniotic fluid.

•

One day, I bring the baby to the sea. It doesn't rain and I'm disappointed. He sleeps in the sling and I look at the blue waves, the kite surfers, the children collecting shells. I'm glad he's asleep; this isn't the sea I want to show him.

•

One o' clock, three o' clock, five o' clock. I open the window. There have been weeks of heat. Sweaty wards. Waking up sweating. Swollen hands and feet. Blood hovering constantly just under the surface of my skin. The heat of healing on torn tissue.

Now, the nights hold hours I have lost. The unravelling of cold, a full emptying and refilling of my lungs, like a dying animal at a watering hole. There is time to listen to the baby's fast and steady breathing, to watch the water fall from the sky in its certainty.

•

I throw away the shields. He drinks for longer. He drinks in his sleep. I open the window so the rain will keep me alert.

Sometimes the rain is so gentle it looks barely there. There are no drops on the glass of the window, but in the crack of light I see it. Swirling in the gusts like dust particles in a ray of sun.

•

As August runs into September, it rains. On the other side of the world the Amazon is burning. The lungs of the earth. We're running out of air.

•

The more I stay awake the less I can sleep. Sleeping becomes abnormal, neglectful.

On still nights, the doors in the sky show the plumb line trajectory of the raindrops. One after another after another. Without the influence of wind, they can't help but fall straight down.

•

Most days I feel like I am, in one way or another, failing my child. If we stay in, I worry he is sheltered, not getting enough vitamin D. When we go out, he may sit in a nappy longer than usual, or inhale fumes while waiting at traffic lights. If I meet every need, I worry he'll be precious. In that way, love itself becomes neglectful. I'm starting to think I'm the problem.

•

I stay up all night. When it grows light, we go for walks. Him, oblivious, wrapped to my body. Around the corner and up the hill. Grey pavements. We walk around the grounds of the convent. Here, the trees are old and there's a smell of home. Pine resin and drizzle. The baby turns his face up to the droplets. The velvet of his brow crinkles. Like everything else, this is new to him.

•

When the baby latches, I am instantly thirsty. It's as if the association of drinking reminds me how little water I've consumed today, like how the sound of waterfalls makes people need to pee. Later, I read that the release of oxytocin causes thirst because women need to drink more to keep up with milk production. I haven't fact checked this yet. I keep forgetting to.

I also forget to fill a glass of water before sitting down to nurse. It's like there's a hole in the pocket of my mind, my only focus is the baby, looking after the baby, everything else (work, wonder, little tasks) is spare change.

At times my let-down, the rush of milk from duct, takes the baby by surprise. When I pull back my breast so he can cough, the milk shoots up, a white geyser, and soaks us both. More often than not I just wear underwear. It's too hot anyway.

The days end prematurely. Heat hangs in the dark. The clouds gather and break. The doors in the sky open.

•

The light inside the house is blue. A duck egg. A bruise. I drive to the sea.

With the baby in the sling, I walk the promenade. He sleeps. The waves roll in and in and in. I taste salt on the wind.

There are people in the water, even though it's autumn now, and the temperature has dropped to single digits. Their heads dip above and below the surface, like cormorants. I imagine the cold coating their scalps with each kick of the swell, the body's involuntary shiver, as if unexpected fingers were running through their hair.

With that kind of cold, you feel the heat in yourself. The inside of your mouth, your stomach. The beat of blood in your ears.

In the sling, the baby stirs.

•

There's a storm. The first of a new season. The wind drives the rain at speed. I rock the baby and hover by the window, opening it just a fraction of an inch.

The rain becomes chaotic. I have to focus to be sure it isn't a blizzard, a sandstorm. The wind is coming from different directions, like sea currents. The movement reminds me of a murmuration of starlings, flying over the dunes at dusk, a thousand individuals moving as one beating wing.

The doorways in the sky illuminate the rain as it falls harder. At my breast the baby sighs. There's milk on his eyelid, smeared on one cheek. The fluorescence catches the sheets of water, turning them white. The slices of light show what's happening somewhere constantly, just out of sight.

+1

I have become the common myth. Mother. The sleepy hum of early memories. The smell of shampoo, of Olay, of lavender. The feeling of safety. The absence of fear.

My body, my life, became the landscape of my son's life. I am no longer merely a thing living in the world; I am a world.
– **Sarah Manguso**

I am a home now. The foundations of a life. Crumble, and untether him into the world.

MOTHER is our point of origin. And when she is gone we are homeless. — **Kate Zambreno**

My life is not my own. My death won't be my own.

0

A category error.
I keep trying to put a shape on it.
Make sense.
    Trying to put words on something pre-language.
    The mind, the unphysical, where the 'I' lives,
gets lost,
travels elsewhere in the body,
and finds it
difficult
to find its way back.

+3

I care about beginnings now.

I find myself googling the etymology of words. The roots of language are not something I had previously thought about. I was the sort of person who said things like *I'm not all that interested in history.* What I meant was I didn't have a head for dates and the people who studied history in college weren't much fun to go drinking with.

Nothing is as long ago as it seemed. Like everyone said, time moves faster than I thought it would.

The future comes at me like a speeding car.

+1

A blackbird has taken up residence in the garden of the derelict house next door. I listen to him sing, wonder if his mate is nearby. There's a sound of traffic. The smell of fried onions travels upwind from the local takeaway.

•

This house I never leave. These months hazy with hormones and flatpack furniture.

Downstairs can be dark; its one long room doesn't get much natural light. That is, except through the lantern. The skylight that arches like a cathedral ceiling above our kitchen. When it rains you can't hear another person speak. I stand under the glass and close my eyes. Imagine the water on my skin.

Lantern, coming from lamp, from the Greek *lampein*: to shine.

I've taken to staring at the sky through the lantern. Watching the swallows loop in and out of view, stray clouds interrupting the monotonous blue.

Sometimes, it feels like we live underground.

•

Outside, the blackbird will not shut up. Even my hairline is sweating.

•

Downstairs, I position lamps carefully around the room. I position lamps to create pools of light. That's what the Instagram infographic calls them, pools of light. *The space is what you make of it.*

•

Moving rooms gives the illusion of time passing.

•

Bedroom shower rocking chair
Bedroom
Shower
Rocking chair
Rocking chair rocking chair rocking chair
Hush little baby hush little baby

•

Moving in space, the space which is what you make of it, brings you through time. Forward, hopefully.

•

From the nursery I watch the sun set and rise. Light taking longer and longer to creep over the rooftops and shine through the glass.

•

The books from my hospital bag, the last things I'd planned to read, are tainted now. They lie in a heap with the leaflets, headphones, handheld fan, water bottle, painkillers, scrunchies, lip balm.

In the nursery: my shelf of poetry books. *I will read them while he sleeps.* My notebooks on the windowsill. *I'll still find time.*

•

Form eludes me. Poetry has lost its meaning. It's too beautiful and dishonest.

These early days, months, everything is hot and loaded. Love and panic. My friend tells me it will fade. Not the love, or the panic, but the intensity. It becomes normal. A new normal.

Like grief, says the baby's father.

•

I become preoccupied with three pieces of art. *Time Lived, Without Its Flow* by Denise Riley, *Ghosteen* by Nick Cave, and *Grief Is the Thing with Feathers* by Max Porter. The first two relate to the death of a son, the latter to the death of a mother to two boys.

I can't engage critically, only absorb. I am all feeling, even when that feeling is not feeling at all.

In these days of new life, I read about death.

Birth is not the opposite of death. The opposite of birth is sex. Birth and death move close together. Parallel lines about to diverge. They tie the mind to the body with more finality than we process in the day to day.

Something so real, so close to not existing at all.

A baby is closest to the elderly, the dying. Where they are going, the baby has just been.

0

Lying on the operating table I think
   I don't want to be here.
I try to focus on the lights, to think of something else.

+1

Even now, weeks later, I am there. The concept of tense has dissolved.

The newborns on the ward were skinny with huge eyes. They reminded me of old men in the final days of life. I could not think of this comparison with my own child, even though he was the skinniest, with the biggest eyes. There was no separation between him and me, between love and pain.

•

When anxiety kept me awake in years gone by, I would write in my head, occasionally jotting words down. Distract my mind until my dry tongue unstuck from the roof of my mouth, and my heartbeat slowed.

My body is overtaking my consciousness. There is no separation between the self and pain. I can't pause this. There is no distraction.

•

The baby's expression suggests agony.

•

I stroke the blue fabric of the book cover. The baby sleeps in the crook of my left elbow. The music plays softly in the background, so as not to wake the baby. I hold the pain of others close. Love brings about a new kind of grief. I need to be prepared.

•

I can't read. I stray away from the construction of narrative. The beauty of metaphor. I try to put a shape on what is shapeless, find structure within the days.

It's not that there's no time.

It's that the old rules don't apply now.

+2

There's a possibility,
that we are among the happiest
people in the world:
mothers.

We're driving from my house to hers when I tell her I'm going to be sick. My knuckles whiten as my mother waits to reach the car park of a country hotel. The car has barely slowed when I fling open the door and vomit straight into a raised bed.

Oh, she says, *I thought you were going to use their bathroom.*

+1

I am not the first woman to have a baby. But I feel like it. I plead with adolescent fury, *You don't understand*. No one told me. No one tells us it will be like this. The world isn't built for us.

0

Pumping milk is, for many women, a sharply private activity. It can also be physically and emotionally challenging, as it reminds the nursing mother of her animal status: just another mammal, milk being siphoned from the glands. Beyond photographs in breast pump manuals (and lactation porn), however, images of milk expression are really nowhere to be found.
– **Maggie Nelson**

•

The baby is in NICU. Every three hours I make the journey from the maternity ward down the endless corridor to feed him. First in a wheelchair, then flinching my way there on foot. The wound in my stomach burns. I want to open it up, put the baby back in, where he was safe. Fifteen minutes before the hour I start the shuffle.

•

They wrap the baby in a blue blanket.
And so, it begins, I think.
I care about beginnings now. How early pink and blue divide. What that means.

•

Alone on the ward, unlike the other mothers with babies snoozing in the plastic crates at their sides. I have books, a small stack I planned to read during all the waiting. I have a notebook I brought with me, but I can't focus enough to write. Besides, I have nothing to say. I read through the thick green folder at the bottom of my bed. The baby has one too. A few days ago, we shared a folder.

Failure to thrive.

I don't know what this means. The baby is smaller than the sonographer said he would be. The on-call consultant frowned, checked his chart. They asked me questions about smoking, drug use, frowned more when I said I did neither.

I think my body was failing to provide him with sufficient nutrients. He was born starving. When the midwife shoved him onto my breast there was nothing for him to drink.

I am failing.

•

My mother's mother, Mamó, had five of her six babies in hospital. 1960s and 1970s Dublin. I ask her about it, breastfeeding.

It was encouraged, she says.

'You should breastfeed,' you were told.

Yet, this was a time when the formula companies came to the hospitals with free samples.

There was a lot of theoretical goodwill towards breastfeeding. A lot of women would say they'd never manage it without such and such a one. But . . . there were an awful lot more that would say, 'Ah here, give up on that, here's the bottle.'

The rate of breastfeeding in Ireland in the 1970s was as low as 11 per cent.

•

At 8 a.m. on the second morning, three hours since the 5 a.m. feed, the midwife with dirty nails asks:

Why are you here? He had formula an hour ago.

I assume she has confused me with another baby's mother. I find out months later that a brief stay in NICU is not uncommon for smaller babies. That he was not in the danger I thought he was.

My son is breastfed, I explain. I tell her my name, point to his. He has only my name. Though I am married, I have not changed my name, and have been recorded, repeatedly, as single. My decision to keep my identity puts me between him and his father.

Most of the midwives I meet are incredibly kind. Their job isn't just medical, they take on the role of reassurer, of hand holder, of a woman who understands. Thank you cards plaster the bulletin board on the wall in their station.

But this one has taken a dislike to me. My questions, my punctuality. She doesn't look up from the chart as she speaks.

You weren't here, and he was crying through our meeting.

•

Breastfeeding and class were connected as far back as 2000 BC, when the use of wet nurses began. First, for royalty and noblewomen. Eventually, wet nurses were hired by merchants' wives as it was cheaper to hire a wet nurse than to hire someone to cover the wife's role in her husband's work.

In the eighteenth and nineteenth centuries, wet nurses were hired to feed premature, sick, or motherless babies. They worked in foundling hospitals, institutions for illegitimate and abandoned babies, like the one which stood where St James's Hospital in Dublin is now.

In the twentieth century, infant formula became the primary substitute for a mother's milk. It provided a freedom for mothers, especially the ones who worked.

In a world where young women were now free to, expected to, live and work like men, formula put a time limit on the demands of a mother's body.

•

Breastfeeding rates strongly correlate to maternal education and social class. The Growing Up in Ireland study found that 79 per cent of mothers who breastfed had a third-level degree compared to 29 per cent who left school at Junior Certificate level.

•

Mamó says, *Breastfeeding was still something you'd do at home in the bedroom. Not out and about.* There was a freedom to bottles.

It was considered trendy. You could go anywhere with the baby with a bottle! You could go anywhere, you could even be at a wedding.

With breastfeeding, you couldn't feed in public. To me, it sounds like a breastfeeding woman was almost confined to the house.

Breastfeeding, being cheaper (free!), was for poor people.

As well, there was an awkwardness about it. Older women would be inclined to stand in front of you, so that you weren't on view.

There was, in the Ireland my grandmother had her children, an unmistakable shame shrouding breastfeeding. Inseparable, as it was, from a woman's body.

The bottle was a feminist miracle. Women could go anywhere and still keep themselves covered up like men.

•

When my mother had me, in nineties Ireland, breastfeeding initiation rates were between 34 and 39 per cent, and this increased to 51 per cent by 2000. Though compare this to 98 per cent in Sweden. By 2016, Irish breastfeeding initiation rates were 56.9 per cent. Still one of the lowest in Europe.

What is so different about Ireland?

•

Now the bottle of formula is a symbol of the mothers eager to return to a cocktail; the women raised on bottles themselves.

Breastfeeding in public is seen as pretentious, exhibitionist, brave. It is a symbol of the luxury of not having to return to work.

When a woman is called brave there's a whisper beneath the word,

You're so brave. (I wouldn't do it.)

No matter what we do, we're doing it wrong, or for the wrong reasons.

•

In the hospital, breastfeeding is approached with caution. Posters advertise a breastfeeding clinic, a pumping room is available 24/7, formula brands are treated with insignificance. Developments in recent decades are evident. Yet the politics of it is tangible. The odd midwife whispers,

Bottle is just fine, you know.

I wonder if they can see me failing. Their job to mind the mammy as much as the baby.

Or, on seeing me nursing,

Good girl.

It's not condescending. There's a pride to it. Every day, these midwives see the battles of a gendered world playing out across the bodies of dozens of women.

–½

I haven't felt the baby move in a few hours. I google variations of the same question dozens of times. I drink something cold, lie on my side, will the baby to move.

I pace the dark rooms, trying to jiggle him into motion. The house smells of paint and sawdust. Outside, the orange streetlight is menacing. The street is still unfamiliar. The Edwardian houses with bay windows, gabled porches, and low walled front gardens, I could be back in the city. Here, like the last two streets I lived on there, named, in rebellion against its architecture, after a revolutionary. I think of one of my favourite books as a child. It's the witching hour, out there, when anything strange can happen. I tell the baby's father to call a taxi.

We go to the hospital.

The labour ward is empty. The midwife on call brings me into a private room, asks a few questions, gets me to lie down. She is quick to action with the doppler. The whooshing like waves.

The thump thump thump. I exhale.

Baby was probably just asleep. They need rest too, says the midwife. She gives me a cup to pee in and mentions keeping me in overnight *just in case you're worried*. Once in, it's difficult to get back out. I will learn that soon.

The midwife pops out. She's gone for almost an hour.

I sip water from the automatic machine and apologise for getting us out of bed. Down the hall, a moan I thought was bad plumbing becomes louder, guttural.

Now that we're out and about, the baby is giddy. He rolls over and my stomach ripples like a bedsheet being shook out. I cup what may be his head, or his bum.

I say,

I just can't wait until he's out and I can see him. Then I'll be able to stop worrying.

$+\frac{1}{2}$

Sometimes, the let-down of milk causes tears to prick my eyes.
It tingles,
and hormones flood my bloodstream.
I gasp a little.
Like the moment after coming, when the pleasure fades,
your openness to love is silhouetted by the impenetrable
distance between two people, and your absolute aloneness
in the universe.

Egg (~)

They say prostitution is the world's oldest profession, but they haven't counted motherhood.

Every mother is rediscovering fire. Reinventing the wheel. Writing the first clichés.

•

I spent years with the possibility of motherhood. The promise of a feeling of completion. The greatest love. The reaching towards it. Fearing its unattainability.

Now, I fear its loss.

•

When I was a child, we kept chickens. Three hens and a cock. I collected the eggs, three a day, sometimes fewer. Eggs are quite sturdy, really. They need a sharp thwack against the pan to crack.

Once I found an egg without its shell. The membrane whole, unpierced. This had probably happened before, but been crushed by the bird and gone unnoticed in the wood shavings of the coop.

I carried it down to the house. The feel of it, rough but soft, like the underbelly of an animal. I don't remember if we ate it. I remember the smell of raw egg, still warm from the bird's body.

In the years we had the chickens, only one chick ever hatched. That hen nested with three eggs. The other two grew cold.

•

I hold anxiety in my mouth like a secret. It threatens to spill out or be drawn back and choke me.

We are all learning and relearning the same lessons. Nobody told me it would be like this. Or, did everybody?

+4

The air quality. I blow the candles out.

I google it. There's formaldehyde in the furniture. We may as well live in a Damien Hirst installation.

Plastic in frozen broccoli. In the water. Only my breast milk is safe, and even that, laced.

Impurities. Attacking his cells, corrupting his mind.

The art of preservation (+½–+2, ~)

Not to take pictures of one's children, particularly when they are small, is a sign of parental indifference. – **Susan Sontag**

•

Staying home all day I start internet shopping. I buy frames. Dozens of frames. I print photos of the baby and frame them. He is photographed more in the first two weeks of his life than my father was in the first twenty years of his. The frames are piled against walls I can't drill into, as I don't know where the electrical wires are in the new house. *We'll run out of wall space*, the baby's father says, with the wariness of a man who has seen what birth does to a person.

•

No one notices the passing of time like a mother. Grief is a part of the territory. Our babies grow within us to grow away from us, and that is the way it must be. We lose them, and have to wish for it, for that means they are grown and our job complete. But it is still a loss, promised from their birth, and we await it always.

•

I get into the bath with the baby to teach him about water. We live beside the sea, and he must have a good relationship with water. I don't want him to be afraid, but I want him to be careful. This impossible balance I've never managed myself.

His legs, gaining weight and strength, leave imprints on the fleshy skin of my stomach. I notice strands of my hair ringing the plughole.

For the months of pregnancy, my hair grew thicker and longer, my nails clacked on tabletops like acrylics, my skin was blemish free. Beautiful and youthful, with the help of vitamin baby. Now I am brittle, shedding, dry skinned.

•

We practise our grief with agonising love, and fear of every cough, every choppy seaside, every rash, every car journey, every possibility. And we practise by losing ourselves, one strand of hair at a time.

•

When my son is nursing in his sleep, I read recipes on mammy blogs. Not for meals — he consumes only milk, and I am still living off peanut butter toast and cheese strings — but for cosmetics.

There are chemicals, toxins, in the products on the shelves.

The internet says, *Would you put this in your baby's system?* It's a rhetorical question.

I imagine them soaking into my skin, flowing into my milk. It's better, safer, to make my own.

I buy beeswax, shea butter, essential oils. When I should be doing laundry, or reading, I melt oils and butters and make balms and creams.

•

I have become obsessed with the art of preservation.

•

Time shifts for the parent. The linear narrative of a life no longer ends in our own death. The child's lifespan is the focus. The present, the moment to be enjoyed, once the primary focus, disappears as soon as it forms. In the future, where are our children living? Is this land we have carved out for them still theirs? To enjoy any perceivable present, we must know our children are secure in the future.

•

In preparation for an upcoming project, I start to learn about the mapping of Ireland. This is not a process I had ever considered, the first recording. I pore over old maps. See places I recognise with names I do not. Places I hope to visit with my son.

•

The growing block theory of time states that the past and present exist but the future does not. This is the theory of time that adheres most closely to what we call common sense.

•

Some mothers experience phantom kicks for years post-partum. The body's remembering.

•

There is a double function of maps. A two-sided coin of preservation and planning. One purpose for the past, one for the future. No thought for the present. The map maker shows you where to go, and where others have been. We preserve to plan, plan to preserve.

•

For the parent, multiple futures exist, simultaneously. Each possible life your child may have.

•

How would maps look if they showed every variation of our country? Every place name, all debated borders, land where now there is sea. Layer on layer, like body on bones.

•

Visiting my parents, I go shopping in the town where I spent my adolescence. I walk to the green. There I ran as a child. As a teenager smoked on the benches. Two weeks from now I walk with the baby's father under the street-lamps, after our first post-baby date. Somewhere in the future, I kick a ball with my son on this same grass.

•

Where the baby's feet used to tuck under my elbow, now they stretch over the arm of the rocking chair as he nurses. He only wakes once in the night for feeds.

•

As we panic, we preserve. A society is a collection of pres-ervations. Buildings, roads, bridges. Technology has given the individual the power of archivist. Selfies, photographs, blogs. We must prove we were here. We must leave our mark. We build. We produce to preserve.

•

Somewhere in the past every parent's child is still a child.

•

My son starts to smile. A social smile, it's called. Babies can smile when they're born. The muscles work, the body reflexes. But they don't smile intentionally for roughly a month. Then, there is something behind the smile. He smiles at his father's laugh. He smiles when I sing. We talk to him. He talks back. *A-goo.* We say it too, *A-goo.* He is finding his voice. Each week a new noise arrives and replaces the one before it.

•

As a thank you for babysitting, I buy my mum a gift from my son. I write *Nanny* on the envelope of the accompanying card. My handwriting, not much improved from childhood, looks as it did on cards to my dad's mum.

•

We replicate what comes before us. Produce our replacements. That's just biology.

•

To some extent I think we want to live every moment of our lives simultaneously. To be children with our own children. To be parents with our parents when they too are young, confused, trying it all out. Not to leave our babies alone in a world we can't protect them from.

•

In school the questions always came back to bite teachers. There are no greater philosophers than children.

But what do you look like in heaven? How would your granny recognise you as an old woman? What if you die all old and ugly and you're stuck that way for ever?

We were told, in heaven you are your most perfect self. The essence of yourself. The self, preserved for all of time.

•

I look at the baby. His serenity when clasped to my chest. I want to ask him, *Where did you come from? Who are you? What do you know?*

•

In the heart of a city now overpopulated, my grandfather is buried. When my family arranged his burial, the fine print explained it is only a rental. After a hundred years, that I remember, the Church and or state reserves the right to remove the headstone and compact what remains for a fresh burial. Body on bones. Layer on layer.

•

The land I am standing on now had a different name. It will be called something else. It has been called nothing at all.

•

When looking for lost relatives, the church will provide a map from the relevant era. My son's great-great-grandfather is buried in the same graveyard as his son, my grandfather. We have looked but can't find him. The map does not seem to correlate to what we can see.

•

We lay down memory on the landscape. A record of what never really existed outside of the agreed social consciousness. We are a conceptual animal. Is it that we want to lay down evidence of the mind? That *thing* which is so real, yet leaves no corporeal trace.

•

My mother's nose is on my son's face, just below his father's eyes. The smile is mine.

•

I frame photos of my son the day I take them, in case I have forgotten what he looks like by tomorrow. I compile albums to document his childhood so that he can look back on it, as if he could remember it. So that I can look back on it, as if I were still there.

+2

I buy a breastfeeding privacy cover at a well-known establishment that sells baby paraphernalia to middle class mammies. I browse online shops when I can't sleep, trying to find a device or toy or blanket that will transform my life into that of a good mother. I've been getting ads for this item on social media for weeks.

A thin triangle of fabric arrives in a brown envelope. The baby's father holds it up.

This was twenty quid? It's a bandana.

It's not a bandana.

It's a big bandana, but it's a bandana.

It's to hide the baby while he feeds.

He raises an eyebrow, clearly thinking I'm being ridiculous.

I've only just started to feel like I'm feeding the baby sufficiently. Being able to leave the house feels greedy, but I want to step back into the world.

•

The majority of people support discreet public breastfeeding, I read in an online forum. The word pops up, again and again, discreet.

I read articles online about breastfeeding in Ireland over the last three decades. How attitudes change. Consistently,

Irish women who give birth in Irish hospitals have lower breastfeeding rates than women not from Irish backgrounds. What's so different in our culture?

The main reason women gave for choosing NOT to breastfeed was because of embarrassment (31 per cent). The second principal barrier was lifestyle and time issues. Many women in the non-initiation group felt that breast-feeding would be 'too demanding on lifestyle', or 'too restrictive and too time consuming'.

Would it seem so restrictive if it were possible to incorporate it into everyday life? Sometimes it feels like Ireland doesn't notice mothers live here.

•

. . . Negative perceptions of breastfeeding including significant embarrassment issues, even within the maternity hospital setting, remain a feature of studies of mothers in Ireland.

•

Ireland, where women are still figuring out how to own their bodies, unsure if they belong to them at all.

•

I knew I was going to breastfeed. My mother did. I know the health benefits. I don't have a regular job to return to.

I don't even drink anymore. It wasn't a decision to agonise over. I try to use my boob bandana, out and about, in cafes. But the baby doesn't like fabric covering his face and flaps like a cross little bird.

I wear dresses and vests that allow for both easy access and discretion. It never works. The baby pulls away and milk flows onto the cafe floor. Waiting staff are consistently accommodating, but I can't be discreet, I can't balance the baby and unclip the plastic buckle of my new nursing bra.

We walk through town. The baby cries. I've miscalculated, he needs milk. I want to pop my tit out, not care what people think, but one cross look at the moment would be enough to reduce me to tears.

I eye up benches that line the river, the gaggle of teens drinking under a sycamore tree. In the narrow pedestrian street that joins the riverside to the main street, a man is pissing in a doorway. I know if I feed the baby here, standing, more people will stare at me than at him.

I think of all the penises I've seen that I didn't want to see. That I've heard more anecdotes about the rudeness of breastfeeding than the rudeness of flashing.

I whisper hushes to the baby and rush home.

We go out less. It's easier, at home, uninhibited by the convention of decency.

–1

Summer is hazy with the sea mist rolling in from the bay.

Colours are popping. Our town is blue skies, buttery yellow sun. The trees could be drawn by children, their leaves waving ridiculously. The mountains are glorious with their purple heather shading, the green and burnt umber curves.

It's like the saturation has been turned up.

Everywhere, people are laughing.

+1, ~

I'm not sleeping. I walk at the first hints of light. We live on a residential street not far from a national bypass. Two rows of attached houses, one room wide, two rooms deep. The older more expensive houses, the ones with bay windows, make me think of posher parts of London, of class distinctions that feel foreign beyond the pale, even though they aren't.

Everywhere in town there are cars. The roar and stink of them. I think of the baby's tiny lungs and long for the smell of trees and damp cattle that fill the air on similar mornings in the country.

It feels illicit, sneaking out while all the houses are quiet, the baby tied to my chest. He's so small, he might not be spotted. I just look like a lone woman in the predawn, walking to nowhere.

When I leave the house, I can turn right or left. Right, and I will be on the route to town, the rush of traffic, sidestepping commuters.

Left, then right, a quick turn up the avenue to the convent. The trees that line the driveway, sycamores, chestnut, beech. Tall, hardwoods. The kind that aren't cut down when money is involved. Old enough to signify that money has been involved here for a long time.

Psilocybin mushrooms grow in clusters, tiny hats on,

huddled low to the ground like they're hiding from the college students who are yet to stumble upon this location. Dew rests on the spider webs that stretch between the strands of tall grass.

The building is over a century old. It hosts crosses, statues, a biblical name. In its heyday it housed the aged, as well as orphans, and poor children.

It makes me think of the buildings like it throughout the country. How many girls found themselves making walks not unlike this one? In trouble, as the euphemism goes. What was their penance?

Though the main building is in the hands of the HSE now, nuns still walk the grounds like ghosts.

·

I read somewhere that it is inappropriate to refer to a mother and her newborn child as two separate beings: they are one, a composite creature best referred to as a mother-and-baby or perhaps motherbaby. – **Rachel Cusk**

In the hospital, after he is born, the midwives use the term and its variants:

Mumandbaby
Motherbaby
Mothernbaby

·

When I check social media, the news is unavoidable. Tuam, the Mother and Baby Homes Commission, the new National Maternity Hospital. Our ever-present history.

To be a pregnant woman in Ireland is to know the fortune of your time and place of birth. If I'd been pregnant a year earlier than I was, I would not have been a priority.

•

The term seems to come from an organisation called The International MotherBaby Childbirth Initiative Organisation. The principles of the IMBCIO are:

1. Women's and children's rights are human rights.
2. Access to humane and effective healthcare is a basic human right.
3. The mother and baby constitute an integral unit during pregnancy, birth, and infancy (referred to herein as the 'MotherBaby') and should be treated as such, as the care of one significantly impacts on the care of the other.
4. Maternity services are essential aspects of healthcare and should be fully funded, staffed, supplied, and freely available to every woman regardless of citizenship or social status.
5. Consideration and respect for every woman should be the foundation of all maternity care.

Later, when my body feels my own again, I will feel at home with this idea, proud and protective. Now, I feel like my body has been stolen.

This defensiveness is my heritage.

•

When I ask her about it, the nuns, the homes, the whole sorry mess, Mamó sighs and says, *A seventeen-year-old leaves school and without any touch of the world decides to become a nun. She has seen nuns always as 'yes sister no sister'. They don't know that this sort of respect has to be earned. So, they put on their habit, and they think because of that, though they have no more wits than any other youngster, that they can be* [redacted].

These lads are only a product of what they'd been made.

I need to remind myself of my luck. The luck of my time, my circumstance.

•

Crows are waking from their roost. Fungi grow as if from fairy tales. Beech nuts crunch under my feet and I can hear the sound of my own breath. The noise of the town feels far away.

This patch of natural world. This solace of green.

In the sling, the baby clings to me. Motherbaby.

Angel's eye, devil's hand (0, +1, +1½)

An angel watches the baby sleep. LED halo and one blinking eye. A sensor connected to the camera lies under his mattress. It detects movement and emits a message to the unit on my bedside locker, which beeps to let me know he is breathing. If the sensor does not detect movement, an alarm sounds. The angel does our watching for us.

Sleep when the baby sleeps.

From the beginning my son is a good sleeper. Yet, I am as exhausted as the mothers of even the most colicky, fretful babies. I sit in the rocking chair in the nursery, the small weight of heat asleep in my arms. Varying, to keep me alert, between watching my son, and watching the summer sky pass from deep blue to the promising pink of another night survived.

·

When did we start needing to monitor everything? Who do I mean when I say we?

·

Before the baby, I was writing about witches and superstition. I am in no way superstitious.

The colonised Irish were seen by the British as superstitious. Barbaric. In history, I'm learning, the powerless are often presented as idiotic.

A popular children's nursery rhyme references the last 'witch' to be burned in Ireland. She wasn't a witch, nor accused of being one, rather she was accused by her husband of being a fairy changeling. Bridget Cleary was a woman killed by her husband in 1895. He served fifteen years.

Her death was used as an argument around the Irish Home Rule issue at the time. It was argued that rural Catholics were too superstitious, and therefore incapable of ruling themselves.

•

The baby sleeps almost seventeen hours a day. I sleep between two and four hours, when I know the baby's father is watching the rise and fall of our son's chest. I make him promise to do so.

•

Superstition is just an illusion of control.

If I sleep tonight, something bad will happen.

•

When they ripped him out of me, they left a mark. Crooked, pink, split at the end where the suturing went awry. A fleshy fork of lightning formed with knife and needle, not hammer and chisel.

•

A devil's mark is the term given to red raised skin lesions that were used as evidence of witchcraft during the Salem witch trials. A brand from the devil's hot claw to seal a deal.

•

In 2012 a woman dies from a septic miscarriage in Ireland. Her death is preventable, by performing an abortion to complete the miscarriage, but the doctors are afraid of the legal ramifications. Neglected, she dies.

•

The anaesthetic fails. Voices grow tinny in my ears. Somewhere, a baby cries.

The patient cannot tolerate the sensation.

The baby produces milk, too, I am told some hours after I regain consciousness. *Witch's milk, they call it*, the doctor tells me. By they, he means not him. A man of science, not superstition.

I have missed the first hour of my child's life. For the first hour of my son's life, I was not watching him.

•

In the nineteenth century, many women were admitted to lunatic asylums due to female hysteria. Removal of the womb was one potential cure.

In 2017, an image listing REASONS FOR ADMISSION went viral. It was from the West Virginia hospital for the insane between 1864 and 1869. The post reported the information to be from women's admissions. Among the reasons were female disease, rumour of husband murder, and superstition.

•

Historians theorise that the devil's marks during the Salem witch trials were actually supernumerary nipples. It was believed the witches' familiars nursed from them.

•

Who's watching my baby?

•

Apotropaic marks are carvings on buildings to ward off evil spirits. The varying shapes include V shapes and crossed lines. They are also known as witches' marks, or devil's marks.

When new mothers say they can't take their eyes off their newborns, they mean it. Not just because the child is beautiful, but because every flicker of eye beneath lid, every soft exhale, every fluttering chest rise, belongs to you. Not in that you own it. Them. This whole small person. But in that they are your responsibility. This new body must be nourished and cared for and watched. This body is yours to love. Unfailingly. Obsessively.

Even when your own body is failing you.

•

I used to make bets with myself.

Laps of the house. Hold my breath. Count the patterns on the wall.

Keep my grandfather alive, my parents happy, let God, if he exists, forgive my unconfessed sins.

As if it were in my control. As if I were responsible for the bad things that happen.

These things we do to keep our families safe. To feel like we're safe.

Don't walk under that ladder. Seven years bad luck for a shattered mirror. Cross your fingers as you say an oath to undo it.

Step on a crack, break your mother's back. Find a penny pick it up, all the day you'll have good luck.

•

This child is all mine to worry about. Because being a child means having someone else to do your worrying for you.

•

A mother is wired to see oncoming threats. If I can anticipate danger, I can prevent it.

•

Sleep when the baby sleeps.

The first night home the baby sleeps in the bassinet in the living room. I sit up to see how he is adjusting to the transition, though he likely knows the sounds and rhythms of this house better than he knew the angry white light of the NICU. This house, where he lived the final months of my pregnancy. He's been here with us. This is his home.

I skip my pain meds in case they make me drowsy.

•

They give me three weeks of pain medication. By they, I mean them, the doctors with the impatience and the shortcuts. I stop taking the capsules the first day home. My body is no longer my own and its pain is largely irrelevant to me now. Now that it is marked by alien changes. The surgeon's slice, the bruises of the needles.

•

We move upstairs the second night. Him, in a bassinet beside the bed. The separation of a few feet feels negligent. To remove myself from consciousness, unthinkable; anything could happen.

•

I keep the baby's arrival off social media. I am afraid of him being watched.

•

He wakes regularly. I take him to the nursery to feed him in the rocking chair. He's asleep again quickly, my skin against his face, milk warming his tummy.

I read articles on my phone about safe sleep for newborns, one arm curled around the silently snoozing infant. More than once my muscles involuntarily slacken and we're both shocked awake.

I am not always the safest place for him.

•

After six weeks, we buy the baby monitor. It's shaped like an angel. A halo of blue flashing light. It beeps, jagged as a failing heartbeat, too irregular to ignore.

I listen to the beeps for the whole night. Watching him anyway, in case they fail to do their job.

Eventually, I sleep for a little longer.

Maybe none of this happened. I've stopped believing everything I tell myself. I'm being honest. But that doesn't mean I'm telling the truth.

+2

The house where I grew up. Home, home, my solid foundation. The kind of security a child needs. Needs to grow. To grow happily. Happily and easily.

It's an hour-and-a-half drive from where we live, my parents' house. We arrive at night, so that the baby will sleep the whole way. I can't handle the idea of him crying in the car, where I can't rock him or soothe him with milk. When he cries, I still feel powerless, panic blurring my ability to act.

The county I was raised in, Mayo, is what my Mamó calls *a big sky county*. Named for the relative flatness of the topography, resulting in the apparent hugeness of the sky. Out here, on a clear day, it feels like you can see the curve of the atmosphere.

At night, the sky is even bigger. The impossible blackness out here is just that, impossible. Smattered with stars.

I step out of the car and it's like breaking the surface. I had jumped off a pier and sunk so deep into the ocean I'd started to think I'd never see the sky again.

On a clear night, like this one, the Milky Way is visible. Here, in the depths of rural Connacht. The great silver brush of it.

I always hated the stars. They invited a kind of existential inquiry that was bottomless. The stars you are looking at are already dead, it just takes the light so far to travel, all that stuff. Looking at them as a child felt like stretching too far to try and reach them and leaving a hollow in my middle.

•

As long as we've been looking up, we've seen that milky smear. As long as the stars have shone on us, we've been nursing our young.

•

In ancient Egyptian mythology the Milky Way was compared to a pool of cow's milk. It was deified as Bat. A goddess that was part woman, part cow. A fertility goddess, a celestial goddess.

•

Across the baby's face, my arms, my clothes. Milk. It sprays embarrassingly.

•

In ancient Greek mythology, Zeus gives his mortal son to his goddess wife, Hera, to suckle. Variations of this myth involve Hera being asleep and not having consented to the act, to Heracles biting her nipple. Either way, she pushes him away and the milk splatters across the sky. The Milky Way.

We are the stars. We are animals, farmed. We are the source of all life. We are convenient nipples. We are gods.

0

Cold where the needle hits skin, then, nothing. Bent over, holding my knees. This is the final stage.

Nearly over now. Hasn't begun yet.

A part of me I didn't know could be felt. Low in my back, like a nail on a chalkboard, but inside me.

Something cold.

Can you feel that?

Yes.

What about now?

No.

Great.

You won't even feel the contractions now.

They come, a line on the black, similar to the heart, and I don't feel them. For the first time in months, I'm not feeling anything.

I don't feel them, but he does. The midwife is frowning. There's an atmosphere of static, apprehension, like the air before a thunderstorm. I pinch my thighs, just to be sure.

You won't feel a thing.

+3

I try to find some motherbaby classes. Yoga, coffee mornings, swimming. Call it what it is, mammy school. School for lost women.

In baby massage class we are asked, *What do you miss about your old life?*

I want to answer, *Potential.*

Instead, I say, *Cigarettes.*

+2

The world is a haze. I grasp at images, words, pulling elements into focus, if only fleetingly.

I can't write.

Without it, writing, I don't know what I am. This isn't an abstract musing. My days won't run, I trip over my thoughts, my body starts to feel clogged up.

I can't think.

The notebook I keep on the windowsill in the nursery is empty, but for a few scrawls. If the baby is asleep over my left shoulder, I can technically write with my right hand. At night, in the smallest hours, I get snatches of peace.

But what comes is unrecognisable. Where has my voice gone?

•

When I write, it reminds me of the absorption in play as a child. Complete and joyous focus on the task at hand. Being entirely present, yet completely away from reality.

Now, I am not a child. The last scrap of childhood leaves as I find myself in a new role: parent.

•

Months from now, in a world as unrecognisable as this one was to me months ago, I will read an article online and come across a word I had not considered. In this article, novelist Anne Enright says, *I felt as you do after trauma: language was no use to me. It has come back slowly, because it always does.*

This can't be a word meant for me. And yet.

•

Not for the first time, I think, did people know it could be like this?

I don't know it yet, but I feel it, this space between trauma and language. When language is what you rely on, what makes you human. When you have been made more animal than human. More body than mind. When the trauma is subjective, internal. When nothing really *happened*.

Time moves differently now. The collision of mundanity and intensity. What shape does truth hold when multiple truths exist alongside each other?

These are the best days of your life.

These are the worst days of my life.

I can't read stories. That used to put sense on my days. I can't write poetry. That once marked my moments as small significances.

In her essay 'Maternal Landscapes' Carolina Alvarado Molk writes, *The format of a narrative presented in fragments, such as Galchen's* Little Labours, *felt tailored to me, to the bits of time that I had for myself . . .*

This is another word that flits into focus. These fragments of myself, of who I used to be. Perhaps there is a language I can speak.

+1

We start to get the hang of breastfeeding. I say we, because he is learning too.

I pump. I want to know the baby is getting enough, so sometimes he drinks from a bottle. The times when I need to sleep for longer than three hours, or be away half a day to teach a workshop, someone else can feed the baby. I don't need to be here at all.

The artificial sucking stimulates more milk production.

This is the first thing I do well. Milk. I can make it. It fills the baby's belly and helps him sleep. I watch a thin layer of fat grow under his skin. I pump more, as if the more milk I produce, the healthier he will be.

Soon, I have an oversupply of milk. This means that I have more milk than the baby needs, and that it comes too fast for him. It bubbles in his tummy, makes him cough.

•

I use a silicone breast pump. It suctions around my breast and the ducts tingle at the force of the milk letting down. Through the clear silicone I see how it sprays like a garden sprinkler. The bottles fill the top shelf of the fridge. Curvaceous. A flock of plastic swans. The first milk of the day is blueish, translucent like Poe's beautiful dead woman.

Later on, as the breast empties, the bottles are topped with a thicker cream separating on the top. Fatty. I imagine a cat sticking her head in a tin pail. There's more than he can drink and it curdles in the fridge.

•

Tiny bottles of formula
single use screw on teats
skinny arms, concave bellies

I look into donation, which I quickly find I am ineligible for due to the medication I am taking for anxiety.

Liquid gold, breastmilk
is called, don't waste
a drop!

I try pouring it into his bath, to keep his skin free of rashes that he does not get, but he starts to smell like cheese, so it goes down the drain.

I find out you can make soap from milk. I order a kit online. The top shelf of the fridge is filled with blocks of breastmilk soap. The baby's father eyes me warily and tells me about a YouTube video he saw where women make bread from their vaginal yeast. It turns out I didn't follow the correct technique; the soap goes rancid within days.

The milk goes down the drain.

I come off the SSRIs that have been swilling around my bloodstream for six years. They're not safe for the baby. The resulting anxiety levels are intolerable. I tell this to the doctor at my antenatal appointment. I am short of breath. A bell rings in my ears. She nods and says something to her colleague. A midwife tells me I'm to be checked in for an overnight. Unplanned, a bed that's not my own, a cannula threaded through the back of my hand.

I run away.

The hospital rings the baby's father. He finds me at home and talks me into going back.

They check me in, and a nurse explains:

It's the only way you get seen, you'd be on a wait list for months otherwise. Bureaucracy, really. Ridiculous.

On a ward with women about to be induced, there is someone talking on the phone about the placenta blocking her cervix, another woman throwing up on an hourly basis. I can still see my toes; I'm not even showing.

I don't want to be here. My skin tries to crawl off and leave me behind.

The next day I'm changed onto medication with fewer associated risks. Nothing, it appears, is risk free.

0

In the hospital, my anxiety is as bad as it has ever been. I'm coiled, fight or flight instinct rushing through me like a drug. I have to explain to each new medic I meet.

+½

Two weeks after my son's birth, I attend a routine psychiatrist appointment. Not for the first time, I don't recognise the person treating me. A locum. I have never met the man who signs my repeat prescriptions.

Without looking at me, he reads on my chart that I am pregnant and asks when I am due. I point to the man pushing the pram in the hall. The locum shakes his head at my notes. He insists that I come off medication immediately. I say no, repeatedly.

Then you must stop breastfeeding.

+1½

At my six-week check-up, the GP is rolling her eyes. My voice is rising, the shake in it cranking the volume up.

She reads me the locum's report:

Patient agrees to gradually come off etc.

That's not what happened, I tell her.

She understands. Never should have happened. Terrible. Going off medication with no warning while two weeks post-partum is, of course, disastrous. Her tone says: What are ya gonna do? She forgets to check my scar. It will be months before I realise this.

+2

My milk is laced with sertraline. My medicated babe.

For the first five weeks of gestation, he grew in a nicotine-soaked body.

Does the steriliser take the microplastics out of the water? Can I purify the air he breathes? Can I keep him safe from the world?

•

This imperfect world I have brought him into.
This imperfect body I have taken him from.

–4

At a writing retreat in Northern Ireland, I am writing a sequence of poems about female suicide in literature. It's a long-held fascination of mine, the chicken/egg relationship between representation and reality for these women. I have to get to the bottom of it, to finish my book, before the baby comes. Before I'm not interested in the same things anymore and my years of obsession are forgotten.

One subject is Charlotte Perkins Gilman, whose suicide comes decades after her mental illness, and is linked to a terminal cancer diagnosis. This feels different than the others, dying before their bodies wanted to, plagued by their minds. I debate whether to include her in the sequence at all.

I reread *The Yellow Wallpaper*, and research her doctor, Silas Weir Mitchell, the physician behind the rest cure. I pull quotes of his from the internet. He told her to live as domestic a life as possible. Not to write or paint. He told her to have the baby with her all the time.

When I first read the story in college, I didn't notice the postnatal elements of the character's suffering, despite it being an integral part of the story.

Now, five months pregnant, it brushes against my awareness, but still, seems irrelevant.

I am still in the before.

I fought pregnancy. It was a thing I wanted, desperately. Then, when it arrived, everything I hadn't done took precedence. I had nine months to get my life in order. Finish books, clear out clutter, learn to drive. It was my biggest deadline.

I took the ease of pregnancy for granted. It wasn't a job, it just was. Invisible labour.

•

At the writers' retreat I tunnel into pages. A manuscript that will be neglected for years to come. I drink when my lips crack a little. In the evenings, the writers dine together. I do my best to partake in chitchat, but my brain is hormone foggy, my thoughts still at my desk.

•

Every hour is closer to time that is not my own. Under my tongue, my heart beats.

The doctor told me to look out for palpitations, lack of foetal movement. My blood pressure has been high. I'm sure my fear of all things blood drives the pressure up when I see the cuff coming to be fastened around my arm. To squeeze until the blood flow through my brachial artery ceases. A diagram illustrating itself in my head until my limbs are shaking, and small stars self-destruct across my vision.

The reading is a self-fulfilling prophecy. My body doesn't seem to know what's good for it.

I'm given things to watch out for, told repeatedly, *If in doubt, come in.*

A mother knows best.

•

I find it hard to trust my instincts. They're usually so wildly wrong.

Writing, editing, reading. Shuffling words and phrases. Hunched over the glass desk so that my shoulders burn when I straighten. I forget to pee, when I leave the room for meals my legs are shaky from being still. I've spent years this way, ignoring my body, its aches and urges. All in the name of art.

I'm still getting used to the rollercoaster flips below my bellybutton. Another thing to block out so I can focus on the work.

Wrapped up in work, I don't feel anything. Then I realise I've felt nothing.

I drink cold orange juice and lie on my side. I go for a walk and play 'Walking on Sunshine' to my belly. Eventually I think I feel something.

There's fluttering in my chest. Fast fast fast. I'm several hours from home, at night, with no car.

Can I be sure that was a kick? Does my heart always beat this fast? Once I get an uncertainty in my head it can be hard to get it out. I've learned to just ignore them. *Nothing is wrong, nothing is wrong.*

Odds are, though, at least some of the time something's wrong.

I google it. Various keywords jumping out. A general message of *better safe than sorry*.

I ring the local hospital to see if I can come in. I just need them to check for a heartbeat. At home, this would be a quick round trip. But, despite its proximity, its similarities, this is another country. The local hospital here doesn't have a maternity ward, and I'm not a patient in their system. It's going to be more complicated.

The NHS sends an ambulance. I tell the woman on the phone that this seems excessive, but she says it's this or nothing.

The paramedic laughs at me. He's an overweight man well into his forties and I can't seem to forget his face. I try to explain I was just asking for an out of hours GP number. I'd been told to always check twice. The paramedic calls me hysterical and laughs again, flirts with one of the other writers who is hanging around to see what's going on. Women and their worrying, he says. He lists the things he's seen as a first responder that are more gruesome than a woman's worrying. I can take an ambulance to Belfast if I insist, he says, but once I'm there I'm on my own. His younger kinder colleague sticks nodes to me for an ECG. I've started to feel the wiggles in my belly again. Everything is fine, I think. It's most likely fine.

The paramedic makes more jokes about pregnant women, about women in general. I cradle my small bump, trust that this man knows what he's talking about.

+6

The avenue curves like an old river. From the hilltop I can see great swathes of the town. How domineering it must have been when it was built, looming over the town like a caution. The hotel feels bigger than the last time I was here, nine years ago, for my debs. At eighteen I couldn't see much further than my own dizzying anxieties, and the bottom of a glass of wine. I knew nothing about it then, its stone towers and twin churches, its history of confinement. Here – before the dressing of stones into luxury, an escape – an asylum.

I am bringing the baby to water. We go underground to a section of the old basement. The windows, far above eye level, show car park shrubbery, disembodied legs.

He wears a cartoon printed poo-catching nappy. I wear the swimsuit I wore on honeymoon. It wasn't new then either. It's a blue polka dot one-piece that plunges at the back. I forget to update my wardrobe. I've never gotten used to not outgrowing clothes. I have to remind myself to replace items long after they've fallen apart.

Parents sit on the side of the pool before plopping in one by one, babies in arms. My thighs flatten and spread. I use the baby to conceal the new folds of my stomach. In the water, he blinks and kicks. He's delighted with this new old sensation. I keep him close to me.

My breasts seem to float, unseemly. The new dads are all topless and smiling in their old bodies. I am the only mum in the pool. The other mums sit in the viewing area, cups of coffee in hands, dyed hair straightened.

At home, I am half-naked most of the time. I wear cotton shorts, loose vests. Some clothing is necessary: cloth to catch the blood, the milk.

Out and about, I wear layers of black. Generously sized, as if I were still pregnant. I cover my body like it's guilty.

But swimming suits like this were made to conceal and reveal all the right parts. Shapely and seductive over function. I am neither naked, like a patient, nor hidden, like I'm on strike from sexuality. My new body has been pushed into its old context.

With the baby in my arms, I move differently in the water.

I struggle to navigate the space my body occupies.

•

We are swimming in the basement of one of twenty-two district asylums built in the nineteenth century to accommodate the lunatics of Ireland. Lunatics, being the mentally ill. This extended to intellectually disabled, unwanted dependants, homeless people.

Now, in my selfishness, I am seeing everything through the lens of a mother. I wonder how many unmarried mothers, women suffering from postnatal depression or even PMS, were among the inhabitants of these institutions.

This asylum closed the year before I was born, then lay

empty, used as a spot for drinking, drug use, and the occasional séance until 2005, when it was opened as a hotel.

•

In the water the baby is free. I hold him around his middle. My role is to support him while letting him explore his body. He can move with a lightness and speed previously unknown to him. When he dips his mouth into the pool, he blows bubbles. The instructor calls him the class messer. The babies do an underwater swim. The instructor explains about reflexes and what our bodies know instinctively but later forget. It's safe, she's telling us. Don't worry, she's telling us. They may be scared, but they won't be in danger. The babies tunnel under one by one. Silence, a splash, a shout of tears. The fathers bounce and cheer them. I wonder if it reminds them of birth.

When my son breaks the surface, he blinks droplets from his impossibly long lashes, meets my eyes with his own, and smiles.

The baby finds only joy in this new sensation. He doesn't fear that his body, or his mother, will betray him.

•

I am trying to be present, but I need to understand. Understand what built the world I'm trying to move through, the world I've brought him into.

How I see this world has changed. The details, the stretch and shift of time, of circumstance, of chance.

•

Ireland has locked away its unwanted for centuries.

It is customary to say we. *We* have locked up our inconvenient people for centuries.

That *we* was British rule, at first. The houses of industry and later the district asylums. Designed, not as locations of poverty and destitution, but places of aid. And later, when the British Empire's influence receded, in swooped the Catholic Church. The Magdalene asylums, industrial schools, the mother and baby homes. Places of charity.

Big Houses for the bodies of the mad, the unruly, the poor, the fallen.

While the powers that be change, we, Ireland, remains. It is honourable to take responsibility for the sins of our communities. It shifts responsibility onto the general population of the past. The past, which includes the victims of the homes, the asylums, the institutions. It's a good reminder. You can be both complicit in a crime and a victim of that crime. We have taught our women where their bodies belong, where the minds of the unwell, the unruly, belong. We have been taught where we belong.

•

In the changing room after class, I take off my togs, so they don't drip on him. I hold a towel under my chin. I can't dress myself until the baby is dry, dressed and in his car seat.

The other mothers are wearing jeans, heavy bracelets, perfume. It is Saturday, the day the dads are off work, and the mothers can wear themselves out like fancy dress. After the swim class, they dress the babies while their husbands dress themselves.

I fail to conceal my body. I am focused on peeling wet clothes from the baby, drying him, dressing him. I am on my knees. He lies on a towel on the floor, and I am thankful that he can't roll over yet. I try not to think of the dirt and shit and petrol residue coming in on shoes.

When I bend too far or stretch in certain ways the nerves within my abdomen burn. Sometimes I look down for the invisible knife. Deep inside me, something still isn't right.

I am folding my body in on itself like a paper boat. This body that has grown and stretched and shrunk. This body that has fucked and wept and been torn apart.

Still there are bruises. Milk falls from me onto the tiles. Though the stiches are healed, the skin at the base of my stomach feels like rubbing velvet backwards: soft, electric, wrong.

+4

There is a discrepancy, between what I thought motherhood would be, how it should look, and how I am experiencing it.

Leaving the house with the baby in the sling, my lower back feels the twinges of the baby's weight. I struggle with shifting the load, tightening straps correctly. I worry about the angle of his hips, his pelvis. The point along my spine where the epidural was administered still aches like a bruise.

I had visions of cloth nappies and babywearing. The baby was going to sleep in the buggy while I wrote in cafes. I'd expected by now we'd be going for hikes at weekends.

I am not the mother I thought I would be.

Though our colouring is different, there's a similarity in our faces, the baby and mine. The shape of our eyes and brows. The same plump lips and chubby cheeks. Mine, babylike, his, belonging to a baby.

I take a selfie with the baby in the sling to send to my mother, to reassure her that we can manage in her absence.

He is curious and turns to look at my phone, changing my expression from pout to smile. In the photo, one of the many thousands already taken of him, his eyes are stormy and inquisitive. The bobble hat confirms that he is, like both his parents, a hat person.

For the first time in months, I look like myself in a photograph.

+6

I will magic myself into a mother. The kind of mother I imagine.

I make lists with the day's tasks. Clean, laundry, shop, cook. Vague enough to leave incomplete.

We walk to Tesco, I on my feet, he in the buggy. I buy tomatoes, broccoli, avocados. I boil lentils, chop onions, look up recipes online.

The baby's father bites into a muffin.

What's in this?

Spinach and sweet potato. Can you tell?

Yes, he says.

My body is a world now. I have to look after it.

In the supermarket, I buy the healthy fats my meat-free diet demands: almonds, avocados, extra virgin olive oil. I don't think of carbon miles, of locally sourced, of blood vegetables. These phrases aren't in my lexicon, yet. I am still in the before.

•

I've been vegetarian my whole life, because I love animals, but a certain amount of cognitive dissonance allowed me to eat dairy and eggs. The eggs, growing up, came from the chickens that we reared and fed. The dairy came from the shops.

It's never been difficult to find someone willing to tell me the failings of vegetarianism. Usually, they're people who eat meat. They take my decision to be a comment on theirs, though really, it's not. It was a meat eater who first told me in distressing detail about the inhumane practices of the dairy industry. When I asked them why, if they knew all this, they still ate meat and dairy, they said simply:

Cause I don't give a shit about animals, and shrugged.

Fair enough, I thought, at least their reasoning follows through.

·

It's not just the suffering of the individual animals that makes the beef and dairy industries so horrible. Livestock emissions make up 14.5 per cent of all man caused greenhouse gas emissions. 60 per cent of this is from beef and dairy.

Climate scientists agree that society transitioning to a predominantly plant-based diet is critical in tackling the climate crisis.

·

I associated dairy with health. An image in my head, a child drinking a glass of milk.

In nineties and early noughties Ireland, where I grew up, The National Dairy Council produced an advert for television on the importance of calcium for children's bones. Specifically, calcium found in milk. In school, each child got a carton of milk a day, decorated with cartoons.

This had little to do with children's health, but rather because:

In 1978, the European Commission introduced a financial support programme to assist the undertaking of national promotional campaigns in an effort to increase dairy consumption and thereby reduce the problem of disposing of surplus milk production within the EEC.

It's the basics of capitalism. Supply and demand. If the demand isn't there, create it.

+7

Babies' stomachs are no bigger than an egg. Their food must be nutritionally dense. Each mouthful justifying the place it is taking that could belong to breastmilk.

Without meat, without dairy, I have to be sure every meal is complex, perfect.

I read avocadoes are a blood fruit. The Amazon is being destroyed for mass soy plantations. Almonds cause drought. The food I prepare for him is killing the planet he needs to survive.

There are too many ways to do it wrong.

I turn to the internet.

I make what the forums call positive changes. I throw out all our single-use plastics. I learn the term single-use plastic. I start to buy our dried goods from a shop that refills your food into jars. I spend hours scrubbing peanut butter from glass corners to fill containers with black beans, rice, quinoa flour, seaweed. The baby's bowls and cups are made of bamboo. They crack easily, but at least there aren't slicks of plastic running from the bottle to his blood.

+2

I am at once huge and invisible. The footprint of the buggy spreads across the pavement. My bum, not insignificant before, has widened and will not shrink.

Yet the world lets us know that we are small. Need somewhere to change the baby, to feed the baby: squeezing into cafes, *sorry sorry sorry*. Receding.

None of my friends are having children. We're only in our twenties. And who can afford to? With rents the way they are in Dublin, and careers in the arts being unreliable at best, but more often than not leaving you reliably broke.

Every time I ask my mother about pregnancy, she says she can't remember. It was a quarter of a century ago, after all.

I download a pregnancy app.

It tells me what size the baby is and will be.

Raspberry, orange, tickle-me-Elmo.

There are forums, a chance to read about experiences from mothers all around the world (though mainly the UK and the US).

Topics seem to mainly include meddling in-laws and a blood test to determine the sex of the foetus. Occasionally a post will appear with the heading

GOODBYE :'(

a story of blood, of cramps, of scans with no heartbeat.

No more to build on there.

These posts always get the most comments, staying at the top of the list for days. Gradually the posts about morning sickness, nursery renovations, and pregnancy supplements resume.

And then, since they

Were not the one dead, turned to their affairs.

Representation (+7, +1, ~)

A photograph is always invisible: it is not it that we see.
– **Roland Barthes**

•

I start to imagine an adult version of my son reading everything as I write it. I project shame and hurt.

Then I feel angry, at myself, at the world. Is it a woman's job to protect men from her potential? Is it not a parent's job to lead by example?

Why do I assume he won't understand?

I want to say to him, I tried my best, and you were only ever a good thing, even on the days I wrote nothing so I could look after you.

•

I keep images of the baby off the internet. His image is his own, and I don't feel like I have the right to share it without his consent.

•

When she's minding him, my mother sends me quarter-hourly photos of my son. Photographs were once a rarity. Now they are a way of being present when you're elsewhere, with almost immediate effect.

Once to travel in time,

now to travel through space.

Photographs are archive (communication with the past, the future!), but also communication with the present.

Teaching a workshop, I pretend to check the time. I get a view into my son's evening with his grandmother. He is sleeping. He is smiling. He is gazing at the lamp. He's laughing. It's like I am there too. I can watch the baby.

But the baby can't find me.

•

My father is a photographer.

My childhood was documented. More so than was common at the time. There are photos of me at every age. I was a cute child, artfully shot.

I grew up a model, one eye on how I was viewed.

Now, I do the same to my son. I am more afraid of forgetting; of not showing him how loved he has been since the beginning.

When I started socialising in my teens, I took photos. I didn't write, then. But the impulse was the same:

[Record create control.]

I took selfies. Photographs of myself, people I spent time with, us together.

I uploaded photographs to the internet. Private photographs, indecent photographs. Not pornographic photographs, but images of intimacy, of friendship, posed adolescents trying to look like they knew how to live.

•

Sometimes I think I have made decisions based on how I imagine them appearing. Not to other people, but to myself.

Does this picture look right?

The cognitive behavioural therapist calls it future predicting.

•

I used to know why men looked at me on the street. There was pleasure in catching the eye of a young, attractive man. I knew I was fuckable.

Now they smile and step out of the way of the buggy. If they see me at all. Mostly they shove past like I am (we are, motherbaby) a wheely bin blocking the pavement.

I am used up.

Single use. Not for resale.

•

All the images of beautiful women I grew up around. Art, photography, music videos, media. Elizabeth Siddal to Kate Moss. Britney's sixteen-year-old belly. Alice Liddell as the beggar maid.

My mother, beautiful in every photograph.

I remember being eight or nine and wishing I was a boy so that I could take photographs of beautiful women. I remember being eight or nine, wondering why men weren't beautiful enough for women to take photographs of them. I remember being eight or nine, wishing I was a beautiful woman who could be photographed.

•

My lovers were artists: musicians, poets, photographers. I exist in a dozen shaky representations. All these men had me in common.

•

In my early twenties I lived with a photographer. Sometimes, he took my picture. At first, I was a willing model. Maybe his skill, his eyes, could make me beautiful.

He was irritated when I insisted on going through the photos, deleting the ones where I looked fat or was pulling a strange face. He was older, and didn't think the model should have a say in the final image. He blamed selfies for making my generation think they had control over their image.

•

I have more than once been obsessed with the biographies of women who were considered muses.

•

The teenage warnings:

Once something is on the internet, you can't get it back.

A girl in school had a naked photograph of her leaked. It was 2008, nude selfies still belonged to the realms of celebrity. I don't remember the boy who leaked it ever being mentioned.

•

I thought I looked better in the photographs I took myself, even when my ex said I didn't look like me in them.

•

Selfies are considered simultaneously a sign of vanity and insecurity. Selfies are considered a feminine obsession.

•

I have been photographed thousands of times. I take more photographs of myself than anyone else has ever taken of me.

It seems, again, to be about control.

•

I won't put photographs of the baby on social media. The internet I spend so much time on. I threaten relatives not to share photographs of him online.

His image is his own.

At a literary event, a photograph is taken of the baby, shared online. I am incandescent with rage, though I know no offence is intended.

My mother reminds me there's nothing I can do. I don't own his image.

No one does. Not even him.

Years ago, I argued with the photographer ex on the ethics of street photography. He maintained that legally anyone could photograph anyone in a public space. I said that the law wasn't the same as right and wrong.

He said something about copyright and ownership. I said something about the right to feel safe.

I phone him to try and remember the details of the conversation. I tell him about the image of my son being shared online. He has recently been asked to stop photographing a seascape because children were playing in the waves.

•

The photographs my mother and I send each other automatically upload to Google photos. They have location embedded in the file.

•

I've always hated being photographed at public events. Reading, or laughing, or talking with someone. Pictures appearing online I didn't know had been taken. I removed tags, pretended the photos didn't exist.

Now, it feels like I shouldn't take the baby places, to keep him offline. Even motherbaby groups post photographs on Facebook.

Can't an experience exist in and of itself without us being reminded of it later?

•

Have I made decisions on how I look? No, how I think I look. The way I imagine I should look. Not to other people, but to myself. I prescribe my life. How should I look, how should my life appear?

Project, imagine, actualise.

How might this look? Is this what a person should do? Is this what a woman should be?

•

I scroll Instagram, see selfies from before the baby, before the move. How pretty I look. I remember the misery then, too. The misery I edited out.

I cut my hair, put make-up on, bite the inside of my cheeks. I take a selfie: windswept, dark eyes.

Do I take a selfie with other people in mind? Yes. But not really. It's *my* reaction to their view that I look for. They don't really exist.

I could be in a hall of mirrors. An infinite number of not-quite-mes. The surface sticky with fingerprints.

•

The Operator is the Photographer. The Spectator is ourselves, all of us who glance through collections of photographs . . .

Taking photographs on my phone. I'm the first to see them. Often, I'm the only one to see them. I'm operator and spectator.

And the person or thing photographed is the target, the referent, a kind of little simulacrum, any eidolon emitted by the object, which I should like to call the Spectrum of the Photograph . .

Taking a selfie, I become both operator and spectator, as well as spectrum. I am the subject of the photograph; the object being photographed.

Entirely self-contained.

●

I keep thinking my observations are original. Only to find it has been said before, better.

I should have been paying better attention.

●

It took me years to read the copy of Barthes my dad gave me. I was never at home in academia. I lacked the patience, the jargon. At that time in my life, I didn't want to read, I just wanted to feel alive.

●

Now, once I feel myself observed by the lens, everything changes: I constitute myself in the process of 'posing', I instantaneously make another body for myself, I transform myself in advance into an image.

When I take a selfie, I contort myself, a mirror that forgives.

Baudrillard's simulacra; the representation of what isn't real.

•

I think my observations are original. As if these thoughts haven't washed over thousands of others. As if any of this is a surprise.

•

My father the photographer. Candid shots of my childhood.
How the baby already notices the dilating pupil of the lens.

•

When people photograph the baby, I am in the background, mouth open, face rounder than I thought, clothes clinging to folds I thought were more subtle. I've never seen myself clearly. I let myself believe the lie I'd designed for other people.
I start to hate images of myself. I start to hate myself.

•

No doubt it is metaphorically that I derive my existence from the photographer.
When the person being photographed is the photographer, is the photographer bringing themselves into existence?
[Record create control.]
When the photograph depends on the object, and the object depends on the viewing of the photograph, the observation by the object itself, of the self, who is the object?

Each time I am (or let myself be) photographed, I invariably suffer from a sensation of inauthenticity . . .

A selfie is a simulacrum: a representation of what does not exist.

•

I'm trying to back up my argument.

I'm trying to prove to myself I'm not alone.

•

In every photograph: the return of the dead.

[Record preserve control.]

I'm not bringing back the dead, I'm trying to protect myself from them. I'm trying to protect us both.

•

My superstition. The marks I make to ward off death.

•

My mother is the photographer now. She takes dozens of images a day on her phone. She keeps a diary. Recording, she calls it.

My father takes 3D photographs of milestone moments.

I think that my son will be able to relive every day of his babyhood by going through the photographs we take of him.

In the early months of his life, I buy albums. I agonise over which pictures to fill them with. How to decide, from the thousands, which make the cut? As soon as an album is full, there are another thousand photographs to sort. It won't be complete until we're all dead.

•

As a kid, when I looked at photo albums of my earliest years, I felt nostalgic, almost sad. Photographs of my mother, my father, me as a baby. We look so happy, I thought, I wish I was there.

I knew, always, that I came from a foundation of love. That they loved me enough to document my every smile.

I want my son to one day visit us in the past, looking at these photographs. For him to know we loved our days with him so much, we wanted to live them twice.

Pregnant, I can't read. The sentences move by quickly but don't stick. I'm too sick to do much other than lie on the sofa, scroll online, fret. I watch films. Rom-coms and dramas. Nothing overly challenging. My mental power feels like it has reduced. I need transient pleasure and a plot that doesn't suffer when I forget the existence of entire characters.

Why is there so much of it? Is there any other medical experience that is portrayed as often, in similar shots that have nothing new to say or show?

Is it the common nature of birth? As many people die as are born. Yet death is shown dramatically (shooting, suicide, accidents), or if it's in a hospital bed, like most birth scenes, it's peaceful, not aesthetically threatening or comical.

In cinema, birth is theatrical. A parody. Sweat all over the woman's face, her biggest drama school screams.

When I see a pregnant woman in the street, I see the pose. Elbows back, knees up, face scrunched. I can't help it. I've seen it so many times.

It's a specific kind of pain porn. We like to see beautiful actresses pretend to be suffering in this way. We like to warn women that their peak point in life is to reach this agonising experience; to bring a baby from their body to the world. To scream, to be out of control in their suffering, to be supported by a man or medical staff.

I wonder will I look that way, make those noises. In the films trying to take themselves seriously, the women don't scream. They low like cows. I think I'm more likely to cry. Pain rarely makes me scream, but almost always makes me cry.

In the back of my mind, I know the world is watching.

+4

The baby is with my mother. I take a train to the city. I was born here. I lived here as an adult for seven years. It's where I wrote, smoked, drank, became comfortable with myself. It has been one of the great loves of my life.

Getting off the train I feel fat, like I smell of money. The remnants of my pregnancy hair is obnoxiously bouncy on my shoulders. My black wool coat brushes the top of my boots. The pockets hold only my phone and wallet. My handbag has notes for my interview and a silicone breast pump to use in the train bathroom so I don't get mastitis.

Usually, in the before, my coat pockets would be full of tobacco, hair ties, loose coins, filter sleeves, house keys, receipts, a leaky pen, maybe a small book. I could leave my flat for the day with everything I needed on my body.

Friends of mine that live here are still broke. Renting or living with their parents. I was the same, before. Before moving to the baby's father's town. His town is the sort of town with several arts festivals, where the cafes all have vegan options, and the teenagers spend weekends in drama groups. There's one homeless man, and everyone knows his name. The drug abuse problems, if they exist, are kept safely in the suburban estates. It's idyllic, where people live when they have figured everything out.

Or maybe that's the only side of it I see. Sober. Married. Maternal.

Now, I crave the dirt and dankness of the city's after hour bars. The sticky pull of chewing gum sticking to the sole of my shoe. The smell of tar, Chinese food, piss. Cigarettes. There's poetry in it. Hope in the struggle.

It's easy to romanticise from the safety.

Four hours and I'm back on the train.

•

His town is our town now, I suppose. Our town is the sort of place I always imagined living. Beaches, craft shops, classes for yoga, Pilates, meditation, organic produce markets, seaweed baths, mountains to hike and lakes to kayak on. It's beautiful. The sort of place someone visualises in a mindfulness exercise.

I call it our town because this is where we live. It's where I'm supposed to feel at home. I call it our town because it's my town now too.

I've been looking up motherbaby classes that incorporate mindfulness, yoga, all that hippy stuff. I imagine myself, cross-legged on the beach, baby in one arm, laughing with other mothers. We're all toned and at home in our bodies.

Maybe, when the baby's older, I'll hike with him in the sling. I can be that sort of person. This is the sort of place I want to feel at home.

–4

He tries to teach me to meditate. Every morning, while I'm thrashing about in the duvet, he meditates in the yard. The American accent of his guided meditation app seems hard to relax to, but it works for him.

The hypnobirthing books talk about meditation. Mindfulness. Being in the moment, in the body.

I try. I do the breathing. It works in that it isolates if I'm feeling hungry, or horny, or tired. I can find desires in my body. I start to think about my teeth.

The voice says distraction is a part of the process. Failure is part of it.

I've never enjoyed things I'm not good at.

It's not working for me, I say. It reminds me of not managing to speak Irish in school. Teachers, my relatives, always insisted I just wasn't trying enough. (A defeatist attitude!) In college, my friend studying ancient languages explained something about verbs, laughed when I said:

I thought you just memorised all the new words.

My brain just didn't work that way. There was something wrong with the click and flow of my head.

+2

The
        baby's
                hair
                        swirls
        night
                like
starry

        Van Gogh's

+1

Sleep is medicine.

Try to watch a film with someone talking to you. Afterwards, repeat the plot, in detail. Frustration. Distraction.

The baby gets used to sleeping in my arms. When I lay him in the cot, he wakes. It has been so long since I had a stretch of sleep longer than an hour, my body does not expect it. The stinging eyes and rolling stomach of exhaustion are not present. I wonder if it wouldn't be better to avoid sleep entirely.

I move through the day distracted, but my thoughts are not elsewhere. Hours elapse and I can't place them. Out of the corner of my eye I am constantly looking for the threat.

+5

My husband's house, our house, is in town. The house belongs to him, though as married couples do, we share. Hopes, anxieties, shampoo, property.

It's a medium-sized town on the west coast of Ireland that I'd given no consideration to before I met him. People from the city come here to surf in the summer. In the winter, the days slip by in perpetual greyness. Grey pavements. Grey sky. Grey haze of smoke outside pubs. I look for the seasons. Migratory birds, buds, browning leaves, the cuckoo.

Because of who I have chosen to share a bed and make a life with, in a matter of months I've gone from poet – scraping by, making a small living from readings, workshops, working in their parents' shed – to homeowner.

Homeowner sounds like someone who can drive and wears 10-denier tights every day. Someone who has a stylist and knows how to wire a fuse. Someone who cooks balanced meals, even if they're the only person home. I am none of these things.

Wife and mother. Homemaker.

For the second time in my life, I am neither employed nor broke. The first time I was a student in receipt of a scholarship. It was more money than I'd ever seen. My job was to read, to write, to learn. To lay the foundations of a life. To indulge.

My time now goes to the baby. Carving out hours to work, to write, must justify his sadness, the moments missed. No one's paying for words that could have been written.

My friend tells her four-year-old she's going for a meeting when she's going on a night out with friends. *It's the only way I can get out*, she tells me.

Work isn't to be enjoyed.

I love my husband more on days when I have written.

When I was pregnant my brain felt foggish, slow. I was easily distracted, like there was someone tapping my shoulder at all times.

Time jolted, stuttered, dragged, and yet slipped through my fingers.

Chopping cherry tomatoes into quarters I think of a sentence. Three hours later, when I go to write it down, it has gone.

Repeatedly, I think of all the things my mother never wrote down. Every time she's said, *I meant to do that.*

And I thought, *Well, why didn't you?*

•

I used to scoff at the country girls who grew up and moved next door to their mothers.

Now here I am, a country girl, desperate to move closer to my parents.

The baby's father doesn't like the countryside. He's from a coastal village close to the country town we live in. I think of him as from the country, an obnoxious habit I share with everyone born in Dublin.

Now here I am, a country girl, desperate to leave the small town.

•

At a motherbaby meeting everyone apologises. The buggies are in the way, the highchairs all in use, the waiter forgot to bring milk, a corn snack is chucked on the floor.

Sorry sorry sorry sorry.

One mother jokes about starting and ending emails with apologies. We all laugh, then nod, smiles half fading.

The baby, once only happy or sad, has begun to express nuanced emotions. The removal of an object he desires results in tears, anguish out of all proportion over a dropped rubber spoon.

The baby gets cross when I look at the computer in his company. Where did he learn that anger? Who told him my time belonged only to him?

+1

Other women tell me things now:

This time is precious.

It will go quickly.

Take me back.

The women tell me:

It's okay to find it difficult.

Men don't understand. They try, but they can't.

You're not going to love every minute.

Everywhere, I see the Marys. Set back in the rock, a grotto, a cave. Like she is some ethereal bear emerging from the depths of a mountainside.

Around where I grew up, when the statues were being put up, they must have been mad for Marys. They crop up at bends on the road, down little lanes, near clusters of houses. The pastel blue and white paint, naff plastic flowers. I drive by on the first sunny day of the year. An elderly woman is out painting the wooden frame of the grotto. She sweeps the brush up and down with her left arm, her right hand holds her lower back. She gives her body, her time, for Mary.

•

The whitethorns are blooming. Delicate plumes. Where you expect to see green, instead there is white. It's a sure sign that we're in May, Mary's month.

It's bad luck to cut down a whitethorn. They're where the fairies live.

•

Mayo is an anglicisation, and no relation to the month of May, or indeed, Mary. But it was here in 1879 that she was seen on the gable end of a church by a young woman, also, coincidentally, named Mary.

•

I find these coincidences everywhere now.

•

In Mayo, you know the change of the months by the flowering of the trees, the fall of conkers, the new calves in the field.

Where I was born, where my mother was born, and where my father's parents were born, is a city. On the cobbled old streets of Dublin town, May was marked with the May parade, the first Monday of May. A parade for Mary.

May Day celebrations in Ireland were largely co-opted from the pre-existing pagan festival of Bealtaine. Bonfires burning to mark the start of summer.

I read up on old stories, recorded in the last century by school children. An archive I return to often, like a family member. I spend hours in conversation with them, though these women were in their eighties forty years before I was born. I can imagine their tones and long inhale before launching into a tale, like my own grandmother.

The baby will come in just a couple of months and there's a thousand things to do. But my ability to hold plans in my mind has all but disappeared. Now, I follow every white rabbit.

Typing keywords into the search bar, I ask them about May.

A Miss Mullalley of Listowel says on May-Eve:

A witch would come in the night on a snare-spancel to every farm house and would milk the cows on May Eve night and when the farmer would milk the cows in the morning and when the farmer tried to make butter out of the milk they could not do it because all the fat was out of the milk. A few years after the farmer used get Holy Water and throw it all over around the house on May Eve and the witch would not come any more.

Customs and suspicions that came down through generations. That were taken less seriously by the time these women were being interviewed.

Mrs Lynch, a farmer's wife, says:

Long ago it was the custom on May morning, at sunrise to bleed the cattle and every person should taste the blood mixed with milk. Men and women were also bled and their blood was sprinkled on the ground.

Milk is mentioned again and again.

Mrs Healy, another farmer's wife, says:

The first three days of May were dangerous for the cows as the fairies had great power on these days, the milk houses were guarded by big bonfires and when the milkman had finished milking he would make the 'sign of the Cross' with the froth of the fresh milk.

The cross, the holy water, living closely with the witches, the fairies. An acceptance of the supernatural, a good magic, a bad magic.

Mrs Healy tells me that:

118

Long ago the Milesians and the Tuatha Dé Dananns had a fight. The Milesians won this battle, and lighted May-bushes were set up in honour of those people. The Tuatha Dé Dananns had a magician, at the head of their army.

One day the Milesians were going to have a fight, and the magician was ready to give the signal until the fight begin. Just as the fight was going to begin, a lighting bush separated the two armies and the King of Milesians was saved.

I note the occupation filled in for these women, 'farmer's wife'. So many of the women full of stories. I think of my own grandmother, the expansive tales she tells me over the kitchen table.

•

The world has become smaller. I want to map it out, see how each thing has roots in something else, a tangled mesh.

•

Every May Day since this a big fire is made, exactly in the same place where the first May bush appeared. All the people bring their cattle through the smoke of this fire, as it was said it used to preserve them from the fairies working any spell on them, Mrs Healy told her scribe.

Do the customs go back that far? The beginning of Ireland as we know it, when the magic was banished underground.

I keep reading. There are half memories of school, of expansive histories from my Daideo. I find myself muttering,

Yes, I knew that, to ease the guilt of my ignorance. Even though there's no one around to hear me.

The Tuatha Dé Danann were the fairy folk. They ruled Ireland before the Milesians, Gael from Iberia, invaded. After the Milesians came, the Tuatha Dé Danann only ruled the world below.

•

The field behind my parents' house used to have a forest of whitethorn. I'm not sure if forest is the right word, I know it's not, it couldn't have been more than forty trees. They sat low to the ground like a hedgerow, but unpruned, their branches knitting into each other.

Other children and I would duck under the mesh of outer thorny branches and into the world beneath. A network of trees that stretched, what was probably not even half an acre but felt endless. Below the canopy the sharp branches were fewer, the darkness there didn't lend itself to new growth. This gave ample room for small children to dash along naturally formed pathways. We weren't to go into the fields when the cows had calves, like they did in May. But once we were under the thorn curtain no cows could get us. You had to be quick though, so the grown-ups wouldn't spot you. Once you were in under the trees, they couldn't get you either. It was a place for small folk like us.

Those trees were ripped up, at some point in the last two decades. The need for grazing more pressing than inherited superstition.

•

Years ago, working on the street my paternal grandfather was born on, I found myself interviewing women from his generation about growing up in the area. They spoke of the Maypole, the Maybush, a walk to the sacred heart statue that was a focal point of the community. We found photographs in the online archive. I scanned every face for features that could be family.

•

In the summer of 1985, Mary statues around the country were reported to move. A friend told me a story about painting one of the statues red. The statue faced their house. He, like many people, hated the Church. He got caught by a trail of paint leading back into his parents' shed. Soon after, he left Ireland for decades.

•

I keep finding connections I'm not sure are there. Links to the world, to the past, where before there were none.

Pareidolia: a tendency to find meaningful shapes where there aren't any. I used to see faces in wallpaper, in dust.

I'd see eyes in the trees, lions in the tint of a car window, a scooter in a spider's web. Eventually it turned into poetry.

•

It feels like Mary is the standard every mother in Ireland is held to. Pure, sacrificial.

•

A year before the phenomenon of the moving Marys, a fifteen-year-old girl, Ann Lovett, died after giving birth in secret at a grotto. Watched over by a Mary statue. Though she died nine years before I was born, every Irish woman my age grew up knowing her name.

•

It is now thought that *Lebor Gabála Érenn*, the eleventh-century book that is the source of much of our country's history, is closer to myth than fact, and was written by Christians rewriting the pagan gods as human, and assimilating pagan culture into Christian ideology.

Their gods became piseóga, superstitions. Passing children and cattle through the smoke to keep the fairies away. When I ask Mamó about May Day and some of the traditions I've read, she tells me that the smoke kept the parasites off the cattle. A practical reason, for it all.

•

It isn't just Mary. It's Mary and Jesus. Mary is nothing without him. Her virginity not as impressive. Mother and son. Our country has hundreds, thousands, of these representations. We grow up looking at a mother adoring her son. At the same mother, holding her dead son, accepting it.

I never realised how much I hate Michelangelo's Pietá. Her passive face.

•

Mary the martyr, Mary sacrificed her body for God, and her son for humanity. The growl in my throat tells me I'll never be divine.

•

Apophenia: a tendency to find a meaningful connection between random things.

•

The whitethorns signal May. Summer. The calves are coming into the fields with shaky legs.

0–1

Portrait in blue:
    The baby's eyes
    The sea
    My lips

I have *bad veins* and a chronic phobia of blood tests.

The response, always the same. Some variation of:

It won't hurt / I'm very good at getting them / Sure it's only a pinch / I had a girl in here who was like you and I got it no bother at all.

Within a few minutes:

Oh, you weren't kidding.

I don't know why it's not on my chart. I know blood tests are important. I know they won't hurt much. Yet, the thought, even the anticipation and

my heart races, my hands shake, my limbs try to run or kick.

As the needle goes in my head splits, my ears ring, I feel like I'll be sick.

My body panics. No matter how much I tell it not to. My body isn't a good judge of character.

I apologise to the nurses. I have a feeling they think I'm difficult on purpose. I ask if it can go on my chart, so I won't have to explain again (so the next person with a needle believes me).

My having bad veins in my arm means getting blood from the blue branches of my hands instead. A teacher in school told us that blood was blue, and only turned red when oxygen hit it. I was eight, and I knew that wasn't the case. Maybe he was thinking of lobsters and hot water.

Deoxygenated blood appears blue through the skin due to the way blue light is reflected.

I don't really understand it, but it's the same reason the sky is blue.

A kinder midwife lets me use a numbing cream on the backs of my hands. Not so as to avoid pain, but so that I might be able to temporarily trick myself into thinking it isn't happening and prevent my system from panicking.

•

For years, doctors have been irritatedly spitting, *It's all in your head*.

The process for coping with phobias seems to be to just get on with it. Power through.

I've run away. I've cried. I've put off tests I needed for years.

•

Well, will you not even do it for your baby? one midwife says. She doesn't understand that she could punch me square across the nose and I may not feel it as intensely as I feel the fear around that needle. But I'm going to be a mother, and mothers aren't allowed to be afraid. I try to separate myself from the sensations of my body's panic. When they take the needle out, I weep. I know that I am fine, but I feel as if I've been attacked.

126

There now, that wasn't bad, was it? the midwife says. She means well. I'm gasping through sobs like a child. It's irrational. I'm angry at myself for being so stupid.

•

Cyanosis is the appearance of blue in the skin caused by low levels of oxygen saturation.

•

Red meat for iron, the nutritionist says. She insists that plant-based iron won't do. I tell her I've never been anaemic before. I eat more eggs.

–1, 0+

The iron supplements make me throw up. I'm given them in advance of the birth, so the baby's iron stores will be sufficient. My iron levels are lower than they, the doctors, would like, and I haven't lost any blood yet.

I take the supplements. Big chalky pills. My body is failing. To make sure my blood is enough, I take pills.

I don't know how much blood I lost; I lose.

Delayed cord clamping is recommended to ensure the blood moves from the placenta into the baby. This can increase the amount of blood in their body by 30 per cent, and prevent iron deficiency, which helps the development of the baby's body and brain.

It doesn't seem like a revolutionary idea, bodies need blood, but I hadn't given it much thought before.

Everything seems to depend on these beginnings. Mistakes are a luxury we can't afford.

The word exsanguinated repeats itself to me.

The baby will have enough iron stores for six months. The baby will have taken what he needs, a midwife re-assures me.

The chalky pills leave me as nauseous as early pregnancy did. I stop taking them regularly. It's easy to let myself forget, now that the baby doesn't need my blood.

Still, I bleed.

+1

Blister packets fall from the cupboard when I open it. Pills big as bees. White, rust coloured, round, elliptical.

The bright yellow of my very own sharps bin, to dispose of the syringes.

Without the surgery, I wouldn't need the needles.

Without the surgery, would either of us be here?

•

I didn't think what it would mean to be a mother in Ireland. How it would make me look at everything differently. Where the roadsides are dotted with the Virgin Mother, and the countryside littered with unmarked children's graves.

I follow my parents through the wood. Past monument and iron gates. Behind anything official. Ivy carpets the ground everywhere except the worn-down track. Here, the trees are a little thinner. Stones, uncarved, rounded only by natural erosion, jut casually from beneath the ivy. There are white crosses on them, smeared as if with fingerpaint.

My mother explains it's a place where babies were buried when they hadn't been baptised. At the time, I think the practice is ongoing. I worry for the souls of the lost babies.

•

Cillíns: unofficial burial grounds for unbaptised babies. They litter the country. Many unmarked, their locations passed down like folklore, known to local people, spoken of quietly.

I wasn't baptised. My own parents having shed any trappings of Catholicism by the time they reached adulthood.

The difference between consecrated and unconsecrated ground seemed insignificant, irrelevant in the face of loss.

•

I ask my Mamó about the cillíns. She tells me that it wasn't just in communal plots, but infants could also be buried in:

The corner of a family field. Very quietly. Consecrated ground was only for baptised people. Unbaptised, and those who died of suicide, weren't buried in consecrated ground.

To me, Mamó is a keeper of the past. Her stories of long ago, told with such clarity. I see them as if somewhere, just a few miles away, these memories and lives are playing out infinitely.

As if the past were one complete thing, and the present another, separate, entity.

This was before. Before time started to simply bleed. Colour running and looping, like milk in bathwater.

Before I felt a version of myself become history, and became a keeper myself.

That there was a world without him, as real and solid in my arms as he is now. My attempts to hold time itself in the forefront of my mind.

It seems ridiculous, to state that lives, and portions of lives, passed are as physical and real as our own. Obvious. And yet, to feel empathy with every person living or ever lived would overwhelm us.

Like the illusion of progress. We assume our civilisation is the best it has been, and only going forward.

So, the past stays safely foreign. Bordered.

The past was easily categorised. I visited it through books, stories my family told me.

Before, when time was linear.

.

It's not enough to say that he is small. That in the past a mother and baby like me and him would not have made it through birth.

·

And if your baby, so small, so dependent. Gone. To let go of the body of your child.

And if all you had was your faith? The only consolation a faint hope of heaven? To take that away?

My pulse is thunderous in my ears. I hold the warmth of my sleeping child close.

·

It all feels close now. Moving shakily behind a closing eye.

+3

Mothers come to me now.

I am not an approachable person. I avoid eye contact with strangers, nod and smile rather than speak if I can get away with it. I like people, I just need warning before interactions, they tire me out. Once, at a writers' retreat on a cliffside, I hid under my table when someone knocked on the door. It had been days since I'd spoken to another person, and I acted on instinct.

I give off every signal I can that says, *Please, leave me alone.* Before now, it had only been men who ignored these signals. Hands on the knee, the small of the back. (*Think you're too good for me? Sure I barely touched you.*)

Now, men give me a wide berth.

At a family member's house, a friend of a relative (I am meeting her for the first time) sits next to me. She squeezes my knee and keeps trying to take the baby from my arms.

Oh, I just need to squeeze the baby, she says, repeatedly. I resist a strong urge to headbutt her. To say, *No, you don't.*

My body is not my own. (Has it ever been?) His body isn't up for grabs.

I think (and feel guilty thinking) that I prefer a man's invasion to a woman's. The devil I know.

Women approach me in public. Overbearing, at times, but mostly cautious, kind. They too have been the touched, the cornered, the new.

They approach the baby, a hand out, a smile.

My boy, he was like that.

Forty-six my son is, can still remember the weight of him when he was that size.

It was hard. When he was that small. People always forget how hard it is.

They speak to me like I'm hearing confession. Like no one else believes that they, too, were new mothers once.

•

We spend Halloween with my mother and her two sisters in my aunt's house. My first cousins are children still. My son is the youngest there, the first of the next generation. All night mums come and go with a parade of small witches, dinosaurs, princesses, vampires, and Buzz Lightyears.

The word bounces around the room like disco lights.

Mammy

Mammy

Mammy

The women refer to each other, and themselves, by it.

Mammy's just going to get the brack.

Mammy is talking to your aunty.

Do you want to have a drink from Mammy?

•

When I was small, I used to say *mammy mammy mammy* to get her attention when we were out of the house. If she didn't respond I'd yell her name, crossly, unable to understand how she couldn't have heard me.

·

One day, you'll pick up your child for the last time, and you won't know it's the last time.

This seems to be a common thing people say to make new parents sad.

Panic, at the thought of losing him to time. Panic, at the thought of not.

I start to think, *One day, I'll hug my mother for the last time.*

Nothing is infinite.

Babies remind us of temporality. Mortality. These truths we live alongside, trying not to look them in the eye.

In the room with the drawn curtains, I know I'm a bad feminist. The blue polyester gown insists on the creases of its folded self. I bat the peaks under my chin down so I can see the screen.

I'm ardently pro-choice. Yet, on the scan I marvel at the instant evidence of *life*. It moves. Like something learning how to *be*.

I feel this is a baby. I know this is a clutch of dividing cells. How can these truths coexist?

I want the right of a woman's life to come above her unborn child's. I want to protect this baby, my baby.

+3

The baby is a few months old. The clocks have gone forward, I think, and the weather is foul, but there isn't yet Christmas stuff in the shops. I walk the nine minutes from our house to the large German supermarket. The baby is home with his father. The public health nurse said it's important for me to get out by myself, *to the shops and places like that.*

The walk is along a stretch of a national road with two lanes. It slices through the edge of the town centre, linking the west to the north-west, and the 'North', meaning the much-debated country.

One strand of tourism for our town advertises it as a gateway town. This makes it sound like a drug, or somewhere you'd only go to leave again. Perhaps that's why the teenagers look so stoned and eager to escape. Not unlike my own adolescence.

There are hailstones. Yes, that was it.

There's no sense in bringing the baby out in that and besides the nurse said you're supposed to be going out without him.

The cars ignore the speed limit. The presence of a town an inconvenience.

One after the other, they veer out of control and flip, throw themselves at the exact spot I am walking by. I am repeatedly smeared like an insect. Blood and milk.

In the blink of passing headlamps the hail is only worsening.

The shop is very bright. Beside the entrance is where they bake the bread. The smell welcomes you in as if in to a boulangerie. It's closer to a cattle mart. Metal, exposed pipes on the ceiling, children rattling the mesh of trolleys like confined calves.

At home the boys must be playing. The boys, this is something other women say about their husbands and sons. The boys. I can't decide if it's affectionate or condescending.

Fall down stairs.

Spill kettle.

Trip on rug.

Leave door open to axe wielder.

Breathing gets difficult. Somewhere around the dried pulses my throat constricts.

When I break through the front door the room is yellow. A nursery rhyme rendition of 'Yellow Submarine' is playing through the Chromecast. The baby's father looks up from his phone, our son asleep beside him. I shake the bags, barely full, from my hands.

+7, –40, 0

It feels like someone has reached out, grabbed my right breast, and squeezed until all the blood vessels burst.

It feels like my breast flew out of the hedge like a pheasant and was smacked by an oncoming van, but somehow survived.

Mastitis. A breast infection most common in breastfeeding women. (And cows.)

I need to nurse as much as possible if I'm to avoid antibiotics and prolonged pain.

The baby paws and mewls like a kitten. He is teething. He gums down on me with force.

I try not to vomit from the pain.

I knead the white dough of my boob. Milk dribbles.

•

It is a spitting grey March day. A beach, a few miles outside of Westport. I am on horseback for the first time since childhood. Mourning an inevitable break-up, I left the smoggy city and travelled west to my parents' place.

It's the day I turn twenty-three and I'm looking to feel something (different).

We take it slow along the narrow coast road, over the marram hillocks. The horses step carefully through rockpools, like women in heels. There's a stretch of beach, the tide is out, with just a couple of inches of water covering the sand. We go from a walk to a trot, then canter towards the far-out waves. The wind is in my face, the horse's mane whips out like strands of seaweed. We turn and the wind chases us, gather to a gallop. The hooves kick up sea water.

The horse stumbles, just a little, at the wrong moment. I rise up in the saddle, and in the split second I should land the horse is lower than expected. A sharp fast fall into the shallow water. Trying to avoid the legs of my companion's horse I drop down, resulting instead in going under my own horse.

He moves over me quickly, heavily. Winded, the few inches of salt water burns cold on my face. I gasp, sure I am dying.

•

The morning my milk comes in I'm still in hospital. I'm sharing a room with two other women recovering from c-sections. The bathroom we share is made-for-purpose. A shower, grab rails, a full-length mirror. It has what is becoming the familiar earthy iron scent of lochia, like a fresh kill.

It feels like something is trying to burst out of my chest. In the mirror, above the band of fabric and electronic drain attached to my scar, my breasts hold themselves up like a pair of helium balloons. I call the baby's father in.

They look fake! I look like a nineties pornstar, I say, slightly dismayed. I am not factoring in the barely closed wound, bags under my eyes, unshaved legs, recently inhabited abdomen.

The baby can't latch. The surface of his target too round, too hard. It reminds me of the dog trying to bite a football.

I use the pump in the nursing room. The milk sprays out in several streams. I deflate, slowly. Within three hours I have refilled.

•

The baby's father slides his hand under my shirt but I pull away. He has the confused and slightly hurt expression of a slapped puppy.

Sorry, I say, unable to explain. The baby is six weeks old. I should be better.

It feels as alien to me now as if I came downstairs to find him massaging the steriliser. My body is a support system for the continuous feed, clean, sleep cycle of the baby.

•

The refilling and emptying grows more subtle. Only I see the difference most of the time. If the baby sleeps longer than expected, I wake, spilling pools onto the sheets. After a long deep feed, he pulls his head back, eyes closed, pursed lips smacking, and sighs. The intimacy of the moment catches in my throat.

My breast is temporarily empty. Light. I don't remember them feeling this way before they were functioning as expected. When he takes his last drink from me, and my body gives up its production, I wonder how they'll feel. Words like shrivel and raisin keep presenting themselves, aggressively. I pinch myself and mutter something about internalised misogyny, but it doesn't help the image of a drying fruit.

•

I was nearly killed falling from and under that horse. Luck, water, and flesh prevented any serious damage. That night I looked in the mirror. I could see the route the horse took along my body. His hooves hit my calf, hip, and breast, missing my head by millimetres. While my leg and hip ached, it was my breast and ribs that showed the most dramatic result. A sprawling purple bruise. Pummelled.

I wrote a poem about it that failed again and again to capture what I was feeling. Language fails me. I fail language. We dance again, hoping to get it right this time.

My body held the evidence of its close call. I am flesh. So easily crushed and torn. Shifting continuously on a cellular level. Building itself up, breaking down.

+3

Too tired to cook, I go out to collect dinner.

It's the longest I've been alone since before. It starts to rain. My phone buzzes and I feel the vibrations travel from my pocket to my chest. It's a text from my mother. She's minding the baby and is offering me a lift home. People are running by with ripping Penneys' bags over their heads. Passing headlamps show the heaviness of the shower, drops fat and glossy. I leave the message unread.

The rain soaks through my hair. Water runs down the small of my back, like sweat. I blink into it. Smell the shift in weather mingling with the petrol fumes. The glue holding the soles of my boots together begins to dissolve.

This luxury of self-neglect. Being wet through, like you can't be when carrying a baby. I walk past the open door of a pub and don't rush, let the fog of cigarette smoke hit my face.

When I walk through the front door I am drenched. I tell my mother I didn't see the message.

I go to book a doctor's appointment to confirm.

I think I'm pregnant.

Oooh, congratulations!

Meeting the nurse, I'm making speeches in my head. How presumptuous! With the new legislation in the news this week. The moral weight of good wishes.

But I don't say anything. I'm here for my body, not my politics.

–5, –1, 0

My job is to make a home, now. To be a home. I read up on changing tables, pick out paint colours. Maybe I'm nesting, but like everything I do, it feels more like a combination of procrastination and obsession.

I still don't really believe there'll be a baby.

I attend the hospital antenatal classes. There's fifty women with a two-week window of due dates. The midwife says she's never seen so big a class. We're in a hot room in the lower floor of the building. Wheels of cars go by the window at eye level. Every week someone has to cough pointedly to get one of the expectant fathers to stand up so that a pregnant woman can sit.

·

We attend a class on hypnobirthing. I have always prepared for events by rehearsing the worst-case scenario. This time I want to be different. It will mark a new me.

I want peaceful, wholesome. That's the sort of mother I will be. In a country kitchen with fresh flowers on the table and homemade bread on the lunch plate. The kind of mother who has a fast labour and an hour of immediate skin to skin.

We're informed of the bureaucracy of hospitals. Unnecessary

inductions and their risks. I'm advised to labour at home as long as possible, to focus on feeling relaxed, safe.

She uses phrases like strong, Amazonian, warrior, super-woman. They make me cringe, but I appreciate the sentiment.

We make a list of films we'll watch in early labour. I pack hospital bags. I practise deep breathing.

•

Still, I find the push, the need, to create. To prove myself.

I feel no responsibility for the creation of my baby. I *know* I am responsible, but I don't feel the right to take the credit. I did not build him. My body made him without my input.

•

I keep reading stories about the moment the baby is placed on your chest. The moment that changes everything. Everything I read talks about the importance of skin to skin. Our hypnobirthing coach tells me not to let the doctors deprive us of this.

There's a clear divide, between medical staff and those outside the hospital looking in. Doulas, birthing coaches, other mothers.

Advocate for yourself. You need an advocate.

I start to feel like I'm walking into the lion's den.

I want, so badly, to trust the doctors, the midwives, even the receptionist who gets my address wrong every time. But it is 2019. A year after the eighth amendment is repealed. I have read the horror stories.

146

If things are progressing quickly, easily, you'll probably be fine. If not? Well.

•

I meet my doctor once. I am told she is my doctor. I raise the subject of birth plans, but she's in a rush. I ask if she'll be there the day the baby is born. She says it's impossible to know. Can I meet all the possible doctors who could be there? *No.*

This is nothing like television led me to believe.

I'm not looking for a bond with the person who will deliver the baby. I don't expect to talk to them regularly, or even like them. I just want to know their name.

I had been labouring under the misapprehension that the patient was the focus of the medical system.

•

The hypnobirthing coach tells me childbirth doesn't have to hurt. The pain is a natural pain. That's why induction is so horrifying. She has several children, and seems relaxed in her body in a way I have never been. She advises me to hire a doula to accompany me to hospital. We can't justify the cost, and are vaguely suspicious of hippies.

An advocate, you'll need an advocate, I'm told again. The implication is clear: don't expect to be listened to.

•

In her essay, 'Grand Unified Theory of Female Pain', Leslie Jamison looks at this perception:

A 2001 study called 'The Girl Who Cried Pain' tries to make sense of the fact that men are more likely than women to be given medication when they report pain to their doctors. Women are more likely to be given sedatives. The study makes visible a disturbing set of assumptions: It's not just that women are prone to hurting – a pain that never goes away – but also that they're prone to making it up. The report finds that despite evidence that 'women are biologically more sensitive to pain than men . . . [their] pain reports are taken less seriously.' Less seriously meaning, more specifically, 'they are more likely to have their pain reports discounted as "emotional" or "psychogenic" and, therefore, "not real."'

More recent studies confirm these ideas. In her April 2021 *Independent* article 'Gender pain gap: Why stereotypes are still harming women's health', Amanda C. de C. Williams notes:

Evidence suggests that healthcare staff routinely underestimate patients' pain, and particularly women's pain, based on a number of biases and beliefs that have little to do with their actual testimony.

A study from March 2021, twenty years on from the one Jamison references, found that,

Gender stereotypes are particularly decisive in the estimation of patients' pain. Because of the false belief that women are oversensitive to pain, and express or exaggerate it more easily, healthcare staff, both men and women, often discount women's verbal reports and non-verbal behaviour expressing pain.

In a 2021 article on the fatal consequences of poor NHS maternity services in England, Sonia Sodha explores this perception of female pain, as well as a lack of research in female healthcare, as the male body is seen as the standard. She concludes that:

Failures in maternity care are not just about understaffing and underfunding: they are linked to a deep-rooted societal perception that women are not to be trusted with their own bodies or to be allowed to make their own informed choices about birth.

•

In the hospital I give the midwife my birth plan. I have made copies, as rumour has it doctors tend to lose them.

I talk about skin to skin, delayed cord clamping.

Yes, yes. Standard practice, no cut until the pulsing stops.

I explain I mean delay for an hour or more. Eyebrows raise.

We'll see on the day.

Nothing is new in creation.
None of this is new.
Everything is new.

Midwives, I've come to realise, are quite like mothers. Most of them are ordinary people doing an extraordinary job. But if you get a shit one, it can really fuck up your life.

Remember. You are allowed to withdraw consent. They should be asking to touch you. You don't have to let them do things you're not comfortable with.

I hear stories of botched inductions, infections, episiotomies performed to rescue a doctor's back from pain, unnecessary vaginal exams, the husband stitch (old), asking a husband's opinion on stitches (new).

The day that isn't a day. The day that is several days. The day that doesn't come naturally. The day that I am tired, scared, weak, failing.

•

The hypnobirthing coach said to remember that I'm not asking permission.

I ask permission anyway. I get tutted, ignored.

Once, I scream, shaking, at a doctor who has looked at my chart but not introduced themselves:

Please, JUST LISTEN TO ME.

•

The endless medics who don't introduce themselves. Then try to put their hands on my body.

•

I don't want to do that.

The shrug and the mutters and the *wait there.*

I know what they're thinking: she has no choice. She's difficult.

I've been fighting with authority for two decades. Why can't I just do it?

A month before the birth, in for a scan, for a test of some kind. One of a dozen reassurances.

They want to keep me in overnight. I'm afraid they won't let me out.

I can leave. They can't make me stay. They don't own my body.

I can't fight the feeling that I'm in danger here.

The baby's panicked father rings me, they've told him I'm missing (again). I'm sitting on a bench outside the hospital, wishing I could smoke, bump under hand. Making an enemy of myself. I know I have to go back in. I know I wasn't really going to leave. But I needed to prove that I could, that it was still my choice.

•

The medical language around childbirth makes the woman passive. The doctor or midwife delivers the baby.

Delivers, from where, to where? My vagina is not a letterbox.

The bringing of the baby from the woman's body to the outside world is the work of the woman. The shifting of muscles, dilating, contracting, pushing. All the doing words are the woman. Yet it is the doctor who delivers the baby?

What of the surgical birth? I am passive. I have no role in the birth. The medical team are firefighters, emergency services, desperate to pull the baby from the rubble of my body.

Can you feel that? You can't feel that.

–2

I don't nest like a bird or a woman in a magazine.

Maybe a crow, actually. In my parents' yard is a barn, used by the previous owners for farming purposes; it has over the last twenty years been: storage, Easter egg hunt location, studio, storage, disco venue, studio, storage, wedding venue, storage.

In the top-right-hand corner, there is a small gap in the sheet metal. This gap is seasonal. In the spring, it is prised open by crows, who then chuck hundreds of sticks down the hole. They will do this until they make a foundation firm enough to lay eggs in, like a backwards game of kerplunk. The problem, of course, is that they would have to fill the whole barn with sticks. This is something they seem perfectly prepared to do. So, every spring, my parents have to thwart their efforts, resealing the hole as they make it.

This is the kind of maniacal hoarding I nest with. The renovation of our house took longer than we'd hoped, and I am seven months pregnant when we first spend the night.

Eight months pregnant, I spend four and a half hours wandering Ikea, mindlessly filling the trolley, with the air of a woman who can't remember where she left her keys. My reluctant mother accompanies me to make sure I don't get lost or sit in an Ekenäset and not be able to get up again. I buy cushions, bedding, rugs, light fittings, bowls, candles.

What room is that for? my mother asks as I place a Skurup pendant lamp into the trolley. I shrug. I pick up a huge glass vase. I'll put it in the empty fireplace that we don't have, fill it up with tealights. It will be *cosy*.

Large glass object on the floor? What if the baby falls on it? my mother says. I hadn't thought of that. The dangers that could come from my negligence. Would a pretty house not be enough to keep a baby happy?

+4

Possessions are my problem. Initially, I had thought that the gnawing absence in my body came from not having the right things. The smoothest running buggy, the most educational toys, a sofa that matches the paint on the wall. The dopamine hit of *new*. Now, I realise it's the opposite.

I order two books on minimalism and start two new Pinterest boards. The baby's father has to stop me throwing away the furniture. I keep using the word clutter.

The Netflix woman said it all has to go at once, or I'll never see it through. How did she know about my long relationship with failure?

He argues that the sofa brings him joy. He doesn't like to waste things, he says it's what's killing our planet. He reuses plastic tubs. I remind him about microplastics. We can't tell which of us is taking the bigger risk.

The furniture stays, but I move it around. The sofa facing away from the kitchen. If I can't see the mess, it won't bother me.

•

In the documentary *One More Time With Feeling* (2016), Nick Cave talks about his wife, Susie Bick, frequently moving furniture around the house. He says that moving furniture is the sign of a creatively unfulfilled woman. He doesn't say this. When I go back, later, to check, he says that it's a sign of a woman with untapped creativity. Yet, I remember it as unfulfilled.

•

Home maker.

A popular interior store uses the slogan *Make a house a home*.

The house doesn't feel like a home.

I blame the dust gathering in corners, where my c-section stops me from bending to clean. I blame the clutter. It's the hardwood floors, I decide. Homes have carpet.

I fall for capitalist slogans. I buy eight new rugs.

+6, -96

In this house. This new house of new family. This house of no sleep, of change, of pain, I begin to lose the ability to feel real.

I know this because it has happened before.

The carpet, plush, so new it sheds like a cat when hoovered (the carpet, not the cat), I don't feel it when the fibres press between my toes.

The baby's father kisses me and it's fainter than a dream.

A profound dysphoria. The feeling that what's around me, or what *is* me, is unreal.

I have a problem with images. Prescription, over description.

This isn't how I thought something would feel. Is this how it looks?

•

This happened before.

A campus. Cobbles, leaves. Dusty books. Bus stops. A drinks cabinet.

Things not looking as they should. Needing to fix it.

I have a problem with control.

•

I cut a hole in my foot with my fingernails. Digging through dead skin until I hit pink. Underbelly.

The same fear fuels it. It's going too fast. I'm doing it wrong.

There's a safety in being numb.

.

Depression is a thief. It robs people of different things. For me it is time.

.

I close my eyes now and feel my son's hand on my breast, his breath on my neck, the weight of his little toes resting on my knee. Already he is six months old. I have held him like this for over a hundred and seventy nights. How often have I taken the time to be present, and feel this brief sweet intimacy?

I write because I am afraid. Not of forgetting, but of never noticing. I write to say look, look what you're missing while you worry.

.

The time is coloured with the recurring thoughts of pain, of panic. Warm glows of love lost to nights of despair.

.

I've done this before. I think of college.

Quick. I couldn't read, despite studying English. I couldn't think. The intensity of living only brushed against my consciousness when I was four glasses of wine in. I told three men I loved them, forgetting to notice the feel of skin, the five o'clock shadows, the cigarette smoke, the laughs. When I think of them now, three pairs of arms around me becomes one. I barely noticed it.

•

Anxiety, in the past, kept me from love. Obsessive, intrusive possibilities entered my head. I say entered, though they originated from within, I suppose. Drowning, tripping, stabbing, etc. I decided to avoid the depth of feeling, of love, again.

•

This is not the kind of love I can distract myself from.

•

I hold my breath so I can hear the baby's soft exhale.

Depression is a thief. All depression steals time. I resent postnatal depression the most for the quality of time it stole. I don't remember the smell of my newborn's head. (The baby's father said he smelled like me, except not sexy.)

This is not the kind of love I can deny.

+4

Months are irrelevant until the baby is over twelve weeks. Then, the baby is three months old. Some mothers push it, seventeen weeks, twenty weeks. I expect they'll also be saying twenty-seven months instead of two.

But pregnancy is weeks. Medically speaking. And near the end, it's weeks and days. 38+5, 37+1, 40+4. They let the mothers in on their language, temporarily.

How silly, I think, to try and categorise all that change into such a short space of time. Look, the hours shrink and swell as we grow.

+3

The night hours have long held something different for me. Perhaps I'm wired that way. In the mornings I am groggy, but once the hour is late enough that I should be asleep there's a bright readiness aglow inside of me.

It's when I write. Try as I might to make myself a morning person. I have tried. Alarms and routines and stubbornness. Yet the first few hours of most days are foggy with sleep and a vague anxiety of the day's tasks.

I like the night. The time that's entirely my own. No one needs me. I'm not supposed to be answering emails, cleaning the house, keeping an eye on my phone in case it rings.

•

The baby wakes several times a night. I sit in the rocking chair while he nurses back to sleep. I could lay him back in the cot, snatch another hour's sleep before he wakes again.

He is warm, and slots easily against me. He won't always fit across my lap. I watch his sleeping face, the slightly open mouth and impossibly long eyelashes.

I watch the sky's dependable dark.

My heart beats steadily and I don't think of anything but what is in front of me.

I use a note app on my phone. Tap out thoughts as they come.

•

In my infinite scrolling I read about a phenomenon called revenge bedtime procrastination. A person stays up late to reclaim hours they have no control over during the day.

Nothing here is new.

Again, it's about control.

Before

Over the years I have been diagnosed with depression, general anxiety disorder, panic disorder, OCD. No, I have not. I have been given those terms to try on like ugly hats.

These are not uncommon conditions. I wouldn't with confidence say I have any of them.

I have been unable to perfectly define the array of symptoms that come together to disrupt my ability to function as expected from day to week to month.

An inexhaustive list of symptoms:

Dysphoria, depression, anxiety, intrusive thoughts, obsessive thought patterns and behaviour, paranoia, inexplicable fury, mood swings, fatigue.

I rub up against the world the wrong way.

When I was younger, younger than I am now, though not that young, and I am still, now writing this, not that old. When I was younger, I was sometimes jealous of those with easily identifiable disorders.

Quotidian

When my brain began to stutter away from childhood and into adolescence, I became preoccupied with numbers, repetition, routine. Brushing my teeth, I'd find myself approaching panic at the thought that I would brush my teeth every day for the rest of my life. How many minutes, days, years, to be spent scrubbing teeth?

•

I have a damaged trapezius muscle from spending my teenage years wearing a bag full of too many books and a bra with too much lace. When I carry any weight, or walk for extended periods of time, the muscle swells and grows hot. Physiotherapy hasn't yet helped. It was only in the run-up to ten years of daily pain that I considered it to be chronic.

•

I have tried traditional employment. The sort that involves commuting, suit pants, and a pecking order. Looking at myself in the mirror of a lift, takeaway coffee cup in hand, made me want to hang myself with my bright green lanyard.

I find comfort in the irregularity of the role of artist.

I work in bursts. Fits and starts. During my brief stint in an office, I finished my day's work by 11 a.m. I would then spend hours restless, bored, making tiny paper boats out of yellow sticky notes.

There have been weeks when sleeping fourteen hours and brushing my hair are the height of my accomplishments.

Once, every few months, I get my period. Sometimes, two or three consecutive months. My body, too, recoils from routine.

Recurring thoughts

Love is an animal instinct masquerading as divinity in humanity.
Everyone you love will die. Probably sooner than you think.
This thought, and that one, and every thought everyone has ever
had, is a waste of time.
Time is an illusion.
Suffering is just the human condition.
There's nothing inherently morally wrong with suicide.
You're not even sick, idiot.
They're usually the first sign.

Diagnosis

Diagnosis gave me: SSRIs.

Diagnosis did not give me: therapy, understanding, explan-
ations, healthy coping mechanisms.

Medication seems to work

My first diagnosis as an adult, following three fruitless years of
experience with Child and Adolescent Mental Health Services,
results in medication. This medication coincided with my
coming off the contraceptive pill for the first time in four years.

Two years after my diagnosis I go back on the contraceptive pill. My symptoms return. It is known, I learn, that
the contraceptive pill can cause depression. I stop taking
the pill. My symptoms improve remarkably.

No doctor has ever asked me about the link between the two.

It was 2013. A year after the death of Savita Halappanavar. Abortion was, and would be for six more years, illegal. Savita was refused medical treatment for an incomplete miscarriage due to the presence of a foetal heartbeat. She was seventeen weeks pregnant, there was no hope for the survival of her child. She died of sepsis. Under the eighth amendment, an unwanted pregnancy was not just an emotional trauma, it could be life-threatening.

What doctor, in good conscience, could recommend a young woman in Ireland come off the contraceptive pill?

Recovery

The biggest thing to fear is fear itself.
    In recovery, I rejected fear:
        I walked home alone at night.
        I rode a horse as if I knew how.
        I ignored letters for smear tests.

Hystory

In that viral internet post, reasons for admission included: imaginary female trouble, hysteria, menstrual deranged, masturbation over action of the mind, uterine derangement, women trouble, time of life.

I recoil from any connection between my reproductive organs and my state of mind. Hysteria, the first female disease. Identified by signs of emotional excess. The word comes from the Greek for uterus, *hystera*. The disease can be dated back to 1900 BC when the ancient Egyptians thought it was caused by the movement of the uterus in the body. It was considered an almost exclusively female condition.

Hysteria was perceived differently across the centuries. As a medical condition caused by disruptions to the natural cycle of reproduction (miscarriage, celibacy, menopause, etc.). And as a supernatural problem, caused by sin or possession.

Hysteria is no longer considered a valid diagnosis. The twentieth century brought a fall in diagnosis of hysteria and a rise in diagnosis of depression. It was removed from the Diagnostic and Statistical Manual of Mental Disorders in 1980. Its symptoms are instead thought to belong to psychiatric disorders.

Hormones

My body is as opposed to routine as my brain. I get irregular periods. My hormones peak and swirl and change with no predictability. I can't tell when a mood is a mental health problem, or intense PMS. They are, I've been led to believe, separate problems. This is a binary world.

Pregnant, I feel as furious, anxious, pained, as I was as a teenager. My body holds me prisoner.

I know when it started, around puberty, as my brain fuzzed and I couldn't focus on the imaginary worlds I lived my days in. I clung to each game, each daydream, knowing that one would be my last, watching childhood evaporate from my body as that body changed.

How similar, in pregnancy, my body again swelling and

morphing, my hormones changing. Being unable to write, to think.

It seems the female body, the ultimate creator, is at odds with creativity.

The baby's father talks about meditation and holistic treatment. He has lived half his life with bipolar disorder. There is something feminine in him, in his caring, his anger, his unpredictability. I wonder if that's what attracted me when we met. He understands what it is to live with thin skin close to his heart, back turned to storm waves of emotion.

I wonder at times if I am sick at all. If it's not just the shifting moods of a female body in a world designed for men. Could I just be at war with my surroundings, not the brain within?

You're not even sick, idiot.

+6

The baby's head smells like:
  Salt
  Suncream
  Embers
  Olive oil
  Grass
  Skin
  Very hot sand
  Cream

+2

As the baby nurses, my abdomen cramps, my body trying to find its way back to its old self. I am dotted with lilac, snot green, mustard. Only now, weeks from the last jab, are the bruises yellowing to heal.

After surgery, I need four injections a day to prevent blood clots. Needles bring me out in a cold sweat. An irrational fear. My body reacting to a perceived threat.

The first day or two home, the baby's father injects me. But, as it gets more difficult to find unbruised flesh, I start to do it myself. I don't want anyone else causing me pain. Pinching the skin until it blanches, moving my hand without thinking, a quick prick. I want to be in control.

Recovery is taking longer than I thought it would. It hurts to walk or lie flat. I sit on the sofa, or in the rocker, curled like an animal shielding her underbelly.

Even when he's asleep, the baby prefers to be in my arms. I scroll on my phone. I can't read books, partly because one hand is preoccupied holding an infant, partly because sleep deprivation and pain are affecting my ability to focus.

I scroll on my phone.

I'm not looking for anything in particular, though any information is easy to find, now, with the internet in my pocket. The per cent of the world's rainforests destroyed in my lifetime? One click. Number of extinct species this century? A quick scroll. The number of years humanity has left? Up for debate.

It's not difficult to find information like this, but a certain amount of cognitive dissonance is needed to move through waking hours. Controlling what gets through the filters, the carefully constructed walls.

·

I carry the baby up the stairs. Each step makes me gasp. Even a weight as light as him uses muscles that would rather forget themselves.

I try to stay immobile, distract myself with the screen.

On my phone, I look at maps.

I look at a map of where we live. I look at a map of where I grew up. I look at a map of where I went to college. The dates on these maps aren't the date I am living, but dates thirty, fifty, eighty years in the future. By then, so much of the country is underwater that it no longer looks like our country. Where we live now has disappeared completely.

The baby sleeps against my chest. It is the only place he will still. I sit.

When I am not looking at him, or out the window, I look at my phone.

I read an article about bees.

It's about more than bees.

It's about their decline, their role in humanity's survival, how we are failing them. The photograph at the top of the webpage is a plain of soil, dry and cracked, infertile.

In my chair, the rocking chair by the window, growing grimy with habit.

The cars chug by at all hours. They cough and splutter fumes into the air. Our house has good ventilation. When we leave the windows open, black flecks settle on the inside wall, the sill, the curtains. The fan system whirrs.

•

I've abused my body. Alcohol, nicotine, sugar, lying in bed reading when I should have been out walking, swimming, keeping moving.

It's not like I didn't know what was bad for me. It is easier to feel guilty, to apologise profusely, than to try to be different. I was born into the last dregs of Catholic Ireland. Guilt is as deeply ingrained in our psyche as sarcasm.

My body will fail, earlier than others, earlier than it would have if I'd looked after it. It will fail and I will leave my baby behind.

•

I'm not looking for the information, when I pick up my phone, but it comes all the same. An infographic on deforestation shows the Amazon's green receding against a wave of orange, to black, to brown. The fires rage. For days they trend on Twitter. Articles mention broken records, expert opinions. I forget the specifics as soon as I read them. The scroll isn't made for information retention. The scroll is for impact, an impression.

•

My body didn't react well to pregnancy. It puffed and paled like a corpse. My blood ran too fast, as if I was under threat. The ligaments around my pelvis loosened too much too quickly, like my legs were being pulled from their sockets.

By the end, I was sure I was going to fall apart.

•

Pregnant, I plan to get rid of my smartphone. I don't want my child growing up around screens. But the baby is born, and I don't throw it away. I need the small pleasures of distraction when I am in pain, exhausted, or anxious, which is almost all of the time. Deprived of the nicotine I gave up a year before, and the alcohol I gave up three years before, I rely on the hit of the scroll.

Because my phone is so smart, it tells me the articles I might like to read before I have read them. The articles I'm not looking for.

Articles about bees, about biodiversity, about pollution, about alternative power sources, about nuclear power, about nuclear war, about the apocalypse.

•

My body has been little more than a means to move my mind around. At least, that's how I've seen it, however subconsciously. Neglecting my physical health didn't feel like self-abuse. What was my body to me? My mind was my real place of residence. My body was just a vessel.

Perhaps it was a kind of defensiveness. As a girl, my worth would be equated with my appearance. I wanted it to be more strongly tied to my mind, my intellect, my personality.

My body came to my attention the first time my mind failed me. I was in my teens, and decided that I would find meaning in joy, sensation, presence. My body became a vehicle for pleasure.

I was meditative when I smoked. Slow inhale, slow exhale. I drank to feel like my whole body was smiling. I stayed up all night because that's where you find the stuff of poetry.

•

In the rocker, feet raised, baby (always) asleep on my chest. Settled into a curl that lets the pain alleviate for a while. I scroll. I read.

•

About Hiroshima, about Chernobyl, about the current president of the US hell-bent on the destruction of the human race, about the rising force of the far right, about the sympathisers here in our country, about the history of oppression in our country, the Church's systemic abuse, colonialism. About how everywhere you turn there is the stark and painful evidence of man's inhumanity to man, and now, too, man's inhumanity to earth, which will be the downfall of us all. And now, they're not articles, they're trains of thought, but they're not trains, they're roller-coasters, underground rollercoasters, that zig and spiral and dive through rock and under rivers. They move like water through soil, rushing into every crack, every weakness, soaking into the land primed for them.

•

Pleasure and care are not the same. While my body was doing me favours, I indulged. The rest of the time, I ignored it. I did not equip my body for work, for suffering, and it began to fail under the strain, and my mind with it.

•

There's something not right.

I ask the public health nurse to check my scar. I'm sure there are holes in it, filling with hot oil. Maybe infection is spreading between the layers, where the knife sliced, the gloved hands tugged. Parts of the body human fingers weren't meant to touch. I'm convinced the cut layers aren't joining back together. My body never learned how to heal.

The public health nurse is slim, blonde. She is kind. She is older than me but looks younger. She examines me briefly, stretching the skin with manicured nails. She tells me that the wound looks to be healing perfectly. I want to tell her that the outside looks fine, that's just skin, but it's the layers, deeper down, that are causing trouble.

•

I don't know if I was addicted to alcohol or if I was addicted to escapism. I stopped drinking when it stopped making me happy. I wasn't happy because alcohol made me a dickhead. I didn't like spending time with myself when drunk, or inflicting that version of myself on other people. I stopped drinking because I was happier without it.

I was addicted to smoking. Not just nicotine. To the act. The ritual of it. Still, in my dreams, I smoke. I stopped smoking because I was going to be a mother.

•

I read horror stories on forums about sepsis from infected surgery incisions. I thought sepsis was blood poisoning, the rivers of the body turning fetid, spreading infection to every cell.

But it's not. Sepsis is the body's extreme reaction to an infection. The immune system releases more chemicals than it should into the blood. The fight isn't correctly targeted. To fight off the threat, the body attacks itself.

•

Life online is curated. We present a lie, how we want to be seen, how we want to see ourselves. We can choose the media we want to consume, the version of the world we want to see.

Surely, no one really wants to watch the world burn?

Friends around the world upload photographs. Now, Australia is burning. A viral image of a kangaroo, black against the raging orange. Soon, California will be burning.

The climate, the climate, everyone is saying. It seems more real now that it's affecting the rich.

A loud minority shake their heads, deny it. It's easier to deny it. A quiet minority nod their heads, smirk, drill for oil anyway.

Emergency.

We are in a state of emergency.

Emergency means it's almost too late.

•

Pain ties you to your body. A body can only be ignored when it is functioning as it should.

A *difficult* pregnancy.

A surgical birth.

Emergency surgery.

The violence of being so present in my own body, in a way I couldn't control, reminded me that without the body, the mind is nothing.

•

I hold the baby close to my body. So close, every hour, to the innocence (there is no other word) of new life. He is flawless. I need to keep his body safe to allow his mind to grow. I need to care for him in a way I have never cared for myself. To care for him, I need to be here. I need to care for my body like it's new.

•

I look again at the date on the map. By that year, my son will be the age I am now. Our house will be underwater. There will be no bees. The home I obsessively decorate, as if the right colours on the wall will provide lifelong security for my son. That home will not have the power to save him from the political conflict brought about by food shortages and mass migration.

Outside, a bee is bobbing between the two flowerpots on the patio. I can see it from the rocking chair, the window that I sit at like a cartoon villain. I can walk again; the pain fades so gradually it takes me days to realise it is gone. But my body is tired. Or perhaps it's my mind. I am tired.

I spend more of my life on my phone than in my garden.

•

I am pre-programmed. I don't know it. I believe my mind is stronger than my body. I pretend that I am not an animal. I allow myself these little indulgences, this level of naivety.

It's natural, animal, to be hyperaware to any threats to your baby. I think of the cows in the field, the warnings as a child (my mother protecting her child) to never go near a cow and her new calf; she won't know you're not a threat. To the new mother everything is a threat.

180

I go looking for the threats I'll have to fight off. My defences are down. My animal body wants to know where the danger is. My human mind sees more to fear than it can fight.

•

Consume, consume, consume. The earth stutters.

•

Later, I will realise the maps I had found were artistic interpretations, that it's more complicated than our island turning into a thousand tiny islands. I'll know that this is both more and less terrifying. I will be surprised that I didn't check the source of the information I was absorbing. I will stop reading comments and Twitter threads. I will realise that predictions aren't clairvoyant, that the future is malleable, and our species has a responsibility to change its trajectory. My wound will be a scar, I'll sleep five or six hours a night, I'll remember how to read books. I will be able to compartmentalise, later.

•

Worry rips through me like fire across scrubland. I don't sleep. I don't eat well. I forget to drink enough water. My body struggles.

+5

The baby has blue eyes.
Blue, only, not blue.
      Green and grey and hints of gold. The sea's surface.
Changing. Reflecting.
Reflecting and pulling you in.

+6

Walking up the hill to the convent. I do loops with the buggy.

There are other mothers, we pass silently, no nods or smiles. We've begun to think of ourselves as invisible.

•

A woman in a neighbouring city has killed her children.

•

I read a writer's account of hallucinogenic drugs. Mind altering, or rather, clearing. The lifted veil. To get as close as one can to the essence of what it is to be alive, to exist on this earth.

This novel, a thinly veiled autobiographical bildungs-roman, did not hold back. Names were barely concealed, sex was explicit. It looked for the extreme and tried to go there. The influence of Henry Miller, Charles Bukowski, etc. is evident. A male writer can look for the dankest, most perverse ideas possible, to wallow in shock, constrained only by freedom.

•

Where must a person be, to kill their own children?

•

I keep myself distracted with planning. Career, house, marriage. Smaller days — clean the bathroom, prepare dinner, declutter.

Keep the veil down.

•

Everything relates now to motherhood. Of the infinite ways in which we can categorise people, I have come to now think of everyone as either parent or child. Until recently, though deep into my third decade, I was a child. I existed with the serene backdrop of parental safety. My parents could fix anything.

Now I am a parent. I have created life, though I feel wholly incapable of such a responsibility. The God I don't believe in is all knowing, all powerful. This is how we see our parents. Or, at least, how we want to see them.

If life was consciously created by a deity, she is probably wandering through the multiverse with a leaking nipple, trying to remember where she put her shoes.

•

I wonder how many new mothers there are in this town.

They're everywhere. These spectres pushing buggies, bodies breaking.

·

In a world where death is preferable. In a world where the mind has shifted waking life to something hellish, the future an ever-present threat.

The guilt of creation.

To think, *this world is unbearable, how can I leave you in it?*

Instinct to protect so strong, even if that means to save your child from the world, you must remove them from it.

·

I do loops with the buggy. With the baby in the buggy. It's grey. The pavement, the road, the mottled sky. We pass other mothers. I wonder how many of us there are, new mothers, pushing alone through the fog.

·

Writers strive for experience. The most they can feel.

These days I mainly feel tired. It's a relief after panic. Wrecked, I can handle.

·

The baby has sore gums and a sick stomach. He doesn't sleep until two in the morning, then wakes at four and is up for the day. It's just the one night, but I feel like I've been catapulted backwards. My nerves are fraught, my patience gone. I weep over the sink washing teethers, images of violence arrive in my head fully formed. The fence on the roof garden isn't secure, the baby could fall. The baby isn't walking yet, and definitely can't turn a key and open a door, but I replay the scenario in my head repeatedly. After an acceptable number of hours, I shake the baby's father awake.

You need to mind the baby. I need to sleep.

I'm not falling over. I could have a coffee, power through. In college I would have bought a Coke and a pack of cigarettes and dossed the day away, not interested in wasting valuable hungover lounging hours on sleep.

I have been misunderstanding what it is to be tired. Equating a need for sleep with sleepiness. Just because my body can stay awake does not mean I am okay.

My instinct to protect the baby, even if I am the thing he needs protecting from.

·

When extremely sleep deprived, you can become convinced that you are a ghost. There is a disintegration of language and time. – **Kate Zambreno**

My body stays awake, my head is drifting elsewhere, like a car veering off road. Images and anxieties take the front and centre. There are dreams arriving, nightmares.

Imagined grief (+6, ~)

I have rehearsed how to say goodbye.

In my head, everyone is dying constantly.

I don't want to be surprised.

In my parallel world, I live continuously in the first moments of grief.

•

The darkest days.

In every sense.

The windows of the house seem to shrink.

What have I done? I've done something terrible. How could I?

Bringing a child into a dying world. Not just any child, not a thought experiment child, *my* child.

Why him? I cry to my mother. *Why does he have to be born into the last generation?*

Outside, the water gathering in the gutters is rising.

It's not the last generation.

It's dark out. It has been dark for hours.

Why him? It's not fair! I wail. He is the only child of his generation.

I won't be there to protect him. I'll be dead, he'll be alone.

I cry to my mother. I want her to fix this. If she can fix this for me, maybe I can fix the world for him.

He's not alone, she says, *he'll never be alone. We'll make sure he's never alone.*

I want her to say something magic. To change the nature of reality.

The streetlamps could be fire on the horizon.

You don't know what the future will be like.

•

My chest aches like a bruise.

•

Secretly, I have always planned to not outlive my mother for long.

It has been my protection against the thing I fear most (being without her).

Now, I am tied to the earth for as long as I can manage. I have to stay alive. I have to feel it.

+5

Baby toys are made to catch your attention. Stripes and primary colours. Crinkly shiny flaps. Buttons that toot. The whole aisle is like being in a fun house at one of those slightly rusty fairs that came to the car park behind the train station every summer throughout my childhood.

I buy every toy for under-six-month-olds that TK Maxx has to offer.

I tell the baby's father what I have read (on the labels):

The contrasting colours are good for his development.

He'll like to chew on that.

This will get him familiar with music.

Bewildered, he agrees. Anything to keep the baby happy. Anything to keep me happy.

My own parents have always ardently disapproved of falling for marketing.

I explain to them (calmly, logically, in my head) that I'm not falling for it. I know it's likely bollocks. But if I buy the baby all these toys, all the bright colours and cuddly blankets and books that make him flap his limbs like he's a little bird about to take flight, if I buy him these things, it may make up for the emotional neglect. For my sheer inadequacy as a mother.

+7

I call my mother.

Maybe you just say the things other people won't let themselves think, she says.

Oh, bloody thanks, Mum.

+4

The weather stops sweating like a panic attack and starts to feel like gasping for breath under water. It is dark all the time.

The baby is not sleeping well. Wind, or gums, or stomach problems. I don't know. Some babies cry, I am told. He's an especially good baby, comparatively, I am told.

When the baby cries, his expression looks like his heart is breaking.

He gets back to sleep. I can't. Sleep deprivation takes the control from my thoughts. I am behind the wheel, but the car is driving itself. Thoughts jump into my brain as if they have come from outside.

Life is suffering. More pain than anything else.

What right have I to bring a life into this suffering? What have I done?

Is there anything more evil than having a child?

I shake myself, distract myself. I know these depths. But my defences are weak, and the thoughts spread like a rash.

•

I have long, slightly manic, arguments in my head.

The problem is, logically, suicide isn't inherently wrong. (I remind myself logic was the only exam I failed in university.)

If a person's every day brings another wave of anguish, why should their pain be endured?

Existentially speaking, for the individual, there seems to be little to no reason to live. Biological drive to reproduce, the pull and sway of the body. But if we have evolved to use our minds to overcome biology (we fly in the sky, use birth control, surgically change the appearance of our bodies), then why should we continue to live like animals? Live, as if living is the only option. If the amount of suffering outweighs the amount of pleasure (utilitarianism), then surely there's only one option?

The problem is, this sounds like logic.

I try to back my arguments up. I went to college, after all. I won't be led by emotion. If you are an atheist, with no belief in an afterlife or spiritual realm, if you believe there is no indisputable inherent value to individual life . . .

Every life is sacred, say the anti-choicers, the Catholics, the bible-bashing misogynists harassing women outside abortion clinics. It's the insidious phrasing. Of course, life has value, we think. Before realising we're agreeing with the oppression of female bodies and human rights.

Support of euthanasia grows. People who decide, with sound mind and problematic body, that they no longer wish to suffer.

The abortion argument stalls at several points. Is every human life sacred? The pro-choice person could be arguing that the embryo / foetus is not yet a human life. Or they could be saying that no, every human life isn't sacred, life has no inherent value.

With euthanasia, it comes down to suffering outweighing any positive aspects of life.

When we put my childhood dog to sleep, I was twenty-five. The wailing rose up my throat like vomit. It was the right thing to do. She was suffering.

Yet when it's a person . . . is it all that different?

If life has no inherent value. If suffering outweighs happiness. Is there any argument to be made against suicide?

In college, I loved and hated philosophy for the same reason. It reminded me how little I know.

This is not an argument. It's about as philosophical as two nineteen-year-olds discussing relativity over a bottle of budget red wine.

No good arguments are made late at night, under the influence of mind-altering chemicals. Even when the late night is early morning, and the chemicals come from your body.

•

The suicide problem, in the history of philosophy, has been addressed by men. The dominant authoring of history by men is not news.

Albert Camus said that suicide is the only true philosophical problem.

Men have the power to end life. Men start wars. Men commit the most murders. Men have a higher suicide rate.

Women create life. We all come from women.

Can the starting of a life be as immoral as the ending of one?

•

I know my thoughts are not original. There must be someone with answers for me.

•

There's a school of thought, around since ancient Greece, but regaining popularity in recent years, that it is immoral to bring about life. Antinatalism. I am reminded of antenatal. The argument is that we cause suffering by bringing someone into existence.

The argument made by antinatalists is two-pronged. I break it down for myself:

1. Humans are bad for non-humans.
2. Humans are bad for humans.

Climate catastrophe is among the reasons for the growing popularity in this particular philosophy.

If humanity is, overall, immoral, because it is causing damage to the earth, we must then assign some superior moral value to earth without people. Without humanity, the world would have a higher moral value.

Yet, the natural world, in all its glory, is not necessarily a moral place.

Veganism is popular among the antinatalists. The antinatalists claim to want to avoid harm, to all sentient creatures.

Nature is, or can be, a barbaric place. Earth without people would flourish. The oceans would clear up, the skies fill with birds. And lions would tear open the throat of wildebeest calves. Tsunamis would drown thousands, millions, of animals. Suffering would continue. Suffering is not unique to humanity. As it stands, we are responsible for the majority of it, but we are not alone in its creation.

The climate-driven antinatalists hold a belief that humanity is the root of the crumbling earth. Which, to be fair, is a good point. Stopping reproduction and the extinction of humanity that would follow would bring about an end to the climate crisis. But it isn't the only way that would. Humanity is capable of reversing harm, of being a positive force.

Then, perhaps, it is worth considering that to procreate isn't inherently unethical. That the species is not the problem, but the current system we live under and participate in.

•

In my teens, hormone riddled, struggling with the first flares of a genetic predisposition for overthinking, I deliberated over the ethics of being alive and staying that way. I, like other furious teenagers, blamed my parents for my creation. (*I didn't ask to be BORN.*)

Yet I didn't hold myself to the same moral standard when deciding to create life.

One of the arguments of antinatalists is that you can't get consent to bring someone into the world. I never asked my child if he wished to be born. I did not consider him in my decision-making. Because he did not exist. It seemed impossible to consider the potential feelings of a potential person.

If the suffering belongs to the person brought into

existence, the antinatalist argument is dependent on the idea that life is, overall, a negative experience. The bad outweighs the good.

It's a step before suicide. Preventative measures. An existential prophylactic.

Don't let the next generation inherit your suffering, stop them being born.

But, why wouldn't this school of thought extend to non-human life? The futile life of a wild animal. (Hunger, danger, uncertainty.) Of which there would be more, without humanity.

Antinatalist philosopher Peter Zapffe argues that humans have evolved too far.

Feeling of cosmic panic is pivotal to every human mind.

Consciousness, in his view, makes us incapable of functioning as animals. We need something from nature (an answer to our existence) that nature can't provide. We can't handle being able to conceive of our position in the cosmos. We spend our lives trying not to be human.

Most people learn to save themselves by artificially limiting the content of consciousness.

Zapffe argues that the ways in which we spend our lives are defence mechanisms. Isolation, anchoring, distraction, sublimation. Ignoring such thoughts, dedicating yourself to a cause, looking outside of yourself to think of other things, transforming the pain of living into artistic expression.

He remained childless by choice.

Humans comprehend the world and their place in it in a way that other animals can't. Yet, suffering is inherent to existence. Every animal with a central nervous system suffers.

What humans have, which animals don't, is an ability to give meaning to their own lives.

But how can a person not yet in existence give meaning to their life?

What, for Zapffe, are distractions, may be meaning enough. Most people don't kill themselves. Is it enough to think that this means most people are glad they're alive?

Is every baby born a leap of faith?

Logic fails me. My incapability is mounting.

•

When the baby isn't crying, he looks peaceful. He is the very antithesis of suffering. I kiss his head, I've read it makes babies happy, even this young. It's my job to make him happy.

–6

The woman in the seat next to me looks like she's trying to smuggle a watermelon out of a supermarket. I finally understand the phrase *about to pop*.

The greyscale screen moves into action as the sonographer presses my abdomen. Cold. Lunar. That the screen is showing the inside of my body is surreal. This landscape that I carry with me. I don't know it.

A curl of a bean. Movement. A jump.

Heartbeat.

How clever, that it grew a heart, learned how to beat.

That it is an *it* at all. My body carries knowledge I don't understand.

The baby hops again. If it's a baby, yet. It will be, and it has come to be a *he*, and he is asleep as I write, but now, in the past, he is an *it*, and whether or not it is a baby feels unsure in my mouth.

The probe pressing on my stomach looks like an electric razor. I want to bat it away in case the baby feels pressure. I tighten my fists and fight the urge, instead watch the seascape of my insides, my tiny diver going wild.

How persistent, the spring and wiggle.

Instinct (+4, 0, +19)

Instinct.

We are told:

If the baby is sick, you'll know.

Your maternal instinct will kick in.

When a baby is under six months old, the GP will send you straight to the emergency room with any concern. We go so often. It's the first Christmas tree of the year I see.

Years ago, I was afraid constantly. Afraid of losing the person I loved most, my mother. This extended later to romantic loves, an obsessive panic, a conviction we were secretly subject to the imminent mortality of a *Final Destination* film.

When your instinct is flawed, how do you know when to be worried?

A mother's instinct.

•

Sometimes animals reject their young. If the offspring is weak or seems unlikely to survive, instinct may lead the mother to abandon them.

•

Maternal instinct is said to be the strongest emotional bond in the animal (human) world.

·

In the hospital, the baby shakes. He is two days old. I ring the buzzer. I tell the midwife something isn't right.

I'm encouraged to rest, not to worry over nothing.

I tell myself I'm paranoid. A fool.

At the shift change, they take him back to NICU.

I don't want to take the baby home. The midwife with the dirty nails agrees. She writes the word *incapable* on the notes I'm not supposed to see.

·

It's only paranoia if you're wrong.

Since childhood, before I had any bodily reason to suspect it, I knew I would have difficulty having children. I chose to have my first child in my twenties. I didn't want to stack the odds further against myself by waiting.

I am prone to anxieties that border on paranoia. I have to correct myself. It can be difficult to see danger when it's real.

·

When the baby is well over one, but not yet nearly two, I will lose my second pregnancy.

Like the first time, I will know quickly that I am pregnant. A certainty that my body has changed, despite no real signs. The blue cross confirms it.

Within a couple of weeks, I will start to feel doubt. A fear creeps in that I'm not unfamiliar with. It is a feeling I try to teach myself not to trust.

At the first scan, the sac has collapsed, whatever lies within has no heartbeat, perhaps never did. My body will catch up, eventually, and the pregnancy will leave it. But, for now, my body knows no different. Life is determined to continue, even when all hope is gone.

I will cry while the midwife carries the scan out. I will cry though I am not surprised.

I had a feeling, I will say, and she'll look at me like I'm trying to spook her.

I won't just be crying for the pregnancy that wasn't what I thought it was, I will be crying for the confirmation of my fears. There is comfort in knowing I can't trust my own instincts. I've made a deal with the universe: if I live my life in fear then nothing bad will happen.

I will cry because my fear will not protect us.

0

They are close to me. The green gowns, blue masks, hairnets like dinner ladies'. White overhead lights flashing by like headlamps. Hands on me. Eight sets, at least. Wheels, like a shopping trolley.

The motion loses velocity. They flurry above me like magpies on the smeared carcass of a badger.

Where is he? Where is he?

A woman strokes my face, again and again. She doesn't seem to have a reason to be here. The needle in my hand is pulled at. A hand pushes my head back.

I think, over and over:

I don't want to be here.

My body wants to separate itself. The faces close to mine hide smiles behind their masks. They aim to reassure.

I need to find a way out.

It will be months before I find the words. I will never find the words.

•   •   •

I've been treading water, knowing soon I'll have the strength to swim back to shore. But the waves are lapping at my head. When I open my lips to breathe, I taste salt.

I call my mother.

I need to write, to work, to sleep in the mornings. To go home. Home home.

•

I pack bags. I pack my medication. I pack all the baby's clothes.

I have so much stuff, the baby's father makes jokes about me not coming back. He is worried, under it all.

I'm doing what I always do, I am running. As if a place is home to the version of myself that I need to destroy. That things will be easier, better, if I just go . . . elsewhere.

I pack nappies. I pack the bottles and breast pump and steriliser. I pack books in case I remember how to read. I pack the buggy.

I just need to rest, I tell him. It's okay, he needs to rest too.

This particular kind of running isn't reserved for space. I use time, too. I will be *fine* if I can get to X-point in time. Future me will have it together.

I pack toys. I pack Sudocrem. I pack the baby shampoo that smells like honey. We don't yet know that global events will shift our plans so drastically.

He will miss us. I will miss him. We don't know if the baby misses yet. We barely acknowledge the oncoming missing, we're too set on survival.

•

Time has become fickle. I think wistfully of my past self, like an old lover, think maybe *she* was the one who had it figured out.

I pack up any evidence of my existence in this house. Remove the traces of my chaos. This beautiful house we call home. This finely crafted building I am an alien in.

Anything at all, to avoid the intense reality of the present moment.

0

I want to meet him. I need to be here to meet him. I know how important those first moments are. Skin to skin. Here to protect him.

I can wait.

Only white light and pain.

He's so beautiful he's so beautiful, look.

•

Where there should be words, a shallow gasp.

An eclipse.

A pressure on my mouth and nose.

Black.

+8

The baby is eight months old. He sucks on my cheek and has different laughs. The top of his head smells earthy, soft. Sometimes we sleep with our faces touching. I sing to him and he smiles.

The veil lifts for longer stretches and I can face the love. In all its glorious clichés.

Sometimes it feels like I've missed his babyhood. Wrapped in my own imagined grief. This is the way I have moved through large swathes of my life. Never before has the time been so precious, the pain so acute.

+9, –3

My finger starts to mutate. A red dot. It's a little hard. Then a blister, but not a blister, forms over it. It bleeds. I wake in the night and my hand is black, caked as if I'd been digging in clay, but with blood. I get blood on the baby's clothes, through the sheets. It heals for a week or two, then starts to bleed. Again again again.

I don't ring the doctor. I've always had a subconscious aversion to administrative tasks and things that may be good for me. Eventually, my finger starts to hurt. It isn't bleeding, but it seems to be growing.

I ring the doctor.

The doctor doesn't know. This is the same doctor who gave me the diagnosis of *difficult pregnancy*.

I google skin tags, warts, spider bites.

Eventually my mother finds a possible answer.

The tiny nail gun I was given to prick my finger with during pregnancy to monitor blood sugar. I was dismayed, listing the healthy things I'd been consuming (Fruit! Vegetables! And, mainly, not cigarettes).

The act of bringing the minuscule blade to my skin, pressing down, pushing for the blood to bloom into a sizable drop. My body's response: light head, palpitations, nausea. Dry mouth. For the first three days, I cried every time.

Haemophobia: abnormal and persistent fear of blood.

With every new medic it's a gamble on whether or not they'll believe me. Mostly, I feel like I'm trying to convince them of a superstition.

•

I ring the doctor again and tell him about cases of scarred capillaries from finger prick testing. Does he think it could be that? He agrees. A repeated trauma he says. He recommends I keep the site safe from receiving any trauma so that it can heal.

He says *trauma* again, in the way a medicinal practitioner means it. *A physical injury.*

Doctors have been known to say they can't see the body like a person. It has to be a machine. If you think of them as a person, you're more likely to make mistakes. You don't want a doctor who feels too much empathy.

•

My fingertips bruised. As the weeks went on, the pain of the needle on soft broken flesh increased. But, for whatever reason, the panic subsided.

Proud of myself, I showed my purple digits to the doctor. *See, it's not the pain I mind. It's the fear.*

Self-prescribed Hydrotherapy

-12

My water obsession isn't new.

In Sweden, three months before I fall pregnant, I swim in the Baltic Sea.

I'm tired from all the walking and the travelling. The sixteenth-century castle and the submarine museum are doing nothing for me. I decided to give up on culture. I took the bus out to the baths.

The beach seems impossibly long, the gentlest curve. Recognisably earth, but so unlike the jagged rocks of Ireland, unlike any beach I have been on before.

A wooden bridge stretches out into the sea to the pale green bathhouse. The doors split, I go left. Women lounge across the steps, some alone, some with friends. Bellies and bums and nipples. There's no hint of exhibitionism, of self-consciousness.

I wrap myself in a towel and slip indoors to the sauna. The wood is hot to sit on. The air feels like it has already been exhaled. One wall is glass, and out of it there's nothing but the sea. A deep grey, almost black.

Tattoos, c-section scars, stretch marks. A young woman with wet hair scrapes her legs with her fingernails. I notice a few more are doing the same thing. Exfoliating. Renewing the surface of their bodies.

I stay until I am sweating behind my ears. Until the terror of the water becomes too tempting.

The metal steps are rusted, a kind of seaweed that I don't recognise grows up the sides. I am immune to the cold air; the top layers of my flesh have hoarded the sauna's heat.

The water is so cold it burns. Pleasantly so. I am removed from the pain. I feel only the sensation, like rubbing an ice cube all over my body.

The contrast of the heat and the sea.

Out in the water, a pontoon floats. Men clamber up, cajole, dicks flopping proudly. Jellyfish pulsate under the water. Luminous as lava lamps.

Indulgence, purity, pleasure. Extremes. Baring my body, but not feeling exposed. Not caring what people see. A freedom I've never known before.

The soundcheck of an outdoor concert coming across the bay. Instrumental twangs of violins, guitars. Reverberating over the surface of the sea.

The burning burning cold of the water up to my neck. The bone deep flush of heat still in me from the sauna.

The blue of the sky has been eclipsed by a gold sheen.

I feel almost holy.

–7

New Year's Day. I am a few weeks pregnant. Too soon to tell people, not too soon to feel awful most of the time. We go for a walk by the sea in his hometown. I have decided that this will be a tradition. Now, I recognise the creeping coping mechanism of unnecessary planning. At the pier, dozens of people are participating in an open sea swim for charity.

He is smoking. I eye his inhalation with envy. My nausea is reminiscent of a hangover, and a cigarette and can of something fizzy would have been my go-to, a few years before. He has one month until he turns thirty and promises to give them up then.

Next year, I say, *I'm going to do that swim.* I mean it.

When next year rolls around I will not be able to work out the logistics, but I will crave that swim more than the cigarettes.

–6

I read dozens of articles and papers on it.

I think, I say to him, *the general consensus seems to be hot water is safe. It's not possible to increase your core temperature that much from sitting in a bath, at least not for twenty minutes, AND it's only important in the first twelve weeks.*

I think back to seeing a woman, seven or so months pregnant, in the hot tub in our local gym the year before. How I had the instinct to point out the sign that says pregnant women shouldn't bathe in the hot tub, before reminding myself that she was a grown woman who could read, and it was none of my business.

We decide that the warm and cold baths are fine, and that I can sit into the hot bath for five minutes at a time.

Before I fell pregnant, we had planned a winter trip to Budapest. I'd visited the thermal springs some years before, on a subsidised student trip, and wanted to return with this man. The hot bubbling water and the freezer-cold Hungarian air beneath the stars.

Instead, we go to Spain, his family's villa near Malaga. It's familiar, warm, and relaxing. Like a lot of the Costa Del Sol, Benalmádena is a small, beautiful, Spanish town that for several months of the year feels like it's been slapped with a lager-soaked Union Jack.

February is quiet. We eat breakfast outside. Fruit, cheeses, fresh bread. We read in the sun. In the cool evenings we walk the five minutes to the seafront.

On one of the roads down to the marina, lined with expensive restaurants and late-night shops that sell inflatable floating devices and penis fridge magnets, there's a thermal bath facility. The ownership seems to change frequently, and we're not sure exactly which culture they're claiming to be inspired by. The words hammam and baños are both used as the name shifts incrementally with new management.

Turkish bath – hammam.

Spanish for bath – baños.

The plastered ceilings have been designed to look like a glorious cave. Pillars and tiles that separate the pools hark back to ancient Greece. The music playing is distinctly Arabic.

There are three pools. Cold, warm, warmer. The 34 degrees of the warm pool is safe. Soothing.

I dip into the cold pool. Three Spanish women shriek and laugh, sinking deeper into the warm water as if the goosebumps on my arms are contagious.

It's so cold! How?

I shrug. *I'm Irish.*

The man who is not yet my husband can't handle the hot pool, but I crave the extremes. When I submerge myself after the cold my skin tingles. It feels like my skin might vibrate right off me. It's an enjoyable pain. I stay no longer than five minutes at a time in the warmth, aware of the permeation of heat, the pulsing bean deep in my body.

–1

Pregnancy exacerbated the issue with my trapezius muscle. I expect the only thing that will fix it, if it can be fixed, will be breast reduction surgery. I have refused to entertain the idea for the nine years since the issue started as it could affect my ability to breastfeed. Sacrificing parts of myself for my future child. Sacrificing parts of myself for the things I want the most.

From about month four, the pregnancy has been given the official diagnosis by my male GP of *difficult, and probably won't get less so*. He wasn't wrong. Nearing the finish line, I am in constant pain and long only to be suspended, cooled. I sleep on my side and have to switch sides every hour or so in the night, or my hips scream me awake regardless.

Living as a writer involves living inside the head. The mind is my primary tool. This is a luxury I took for granted.

To escape the body, I must ease its complaints. A vessel, for so long, for pleasure, to escape the mind. It is demanding reciprocation.

I'm craving water more than anything. A month or so before the baby is born, we travel north to Donegal to a coastal spa hotel. I spend hours online, again, googling the words 'outdoor hot tub' while in a separate tab searching 'hot tub third trimester safe???'

I lounge in the water of the thermal pool, stand underneath the tropical showers cooling my back. I am weightless, relieved of the ache and tension of my body barely coping. The jacuzzi is on the deck, looking out over the gold beach. The sea, absurdly blue, sparkles from the sunlight. The bubbles bump my belly, I see the baby roll under my skin, wonder whether he can feel the difference.

+1

My mother comes to visit regularly. She helps with laundry, the house, minding the baby. I'm struggling with walking, still. The heat of healing in my abdomen feels more like the continuous presence of a hot knife. I am a magician's assistant gone wrong, stitched back together.

We're deep into August, I'm not sleeping, I think about the climate constantly.

Sometimes, when the house is clean and the baby settled, we drive to the sea. Sometimes, when the house isn't clean, and the baby won't settle, we go there anyway.

I walk the promenade with the baby in the sling. The waves roll in and in and in. I taste salt on the wind. The force of it does my breathing for me.

+3, 4, 5

The initial healing time has passed. Mothers in my online motherbaby forum are starting to fit back into their pre-pregnancy jeans. I still can't fit into my pre-pregnancy skin. The to-do list is endless. Anxiety and depression work shifts in my head. One clocks on and the other clocks off. Sometimes they linger to have a chat and occupy the same space.

Every chance I get, I escape to the sea.

As he gets bigger, the baby dislikes the blusteriness of the seaside trips. He stays in the car with his grandmother. The woman formerly known as mum, now nanny. I, the woman formerly known as me, now mammy.

I walk the promenade. Climb down over the rocks and onto the strand. In the water, surfers appear like seals. There is no swimming allowed on this beach. The presence of a surf board, for some reason, trumps this rule.

Sometime before Christmas I meet another mum. Her child is the same age as mine. We get coffee and the babies eye each other up suspiciously. Our conversations vary from art, literature, sleep routines, and a deep desire to go open sea swimming. It's not just me, then, I think. Other mothers seem to have a similar urge.

+7

I am commissioned to write a poem on the theme of mermaids. It's the first time I've tried to write poetry since the baby was born.

With some research I find local legends of mermaids. They are always roughly the same story. A man sees a mermaid asleep / singing / etc. on a beach. He steals her magical cloak that lets her live underwater. She marries

217

him and has his children. She finds the cape and returns to the sea. In some stories she brings the children, drowning them, in some she leaves them behind, in some she turns them into rocks. Whatever it is, the mermaid is abandoning her family for the sea. (How could she?)

I drive to a castle said to belong to the man who stole her, in this region. He has the same name as the baby's father, which we laugh about. The ruin sticks out into a particularly violent stretch of the Atlantic. The rocks are layered, dark. The topography of the surrounding fields is flat, and the lack of trees makes the place look dead. There's no one else parked in the car park. It snows. For the first time since the week I found out I was pregnant, I'm out in snow. The spray coming in from the ocean is ferocious. If anyone were to talk to me, I wouldn't hear them.

I spend my twenty-seventh birthday climbing a hill to look at stones. My mother waits below with the baby. It's March. Clear skies, crisp air. The seven stones are said to be the mermaid's children. From here she ran to the sea. It's a raised point on the flat fresh fields of west Sligo. It looks about two or three miles to the sea, but from this vantage point it feels like flying would be the easiest route. She ran on legs that weren't hers. Even though it isn't true, I believe it.

+9

The baby didn't sleep well. We're in my childhood bedroom. When morning rushes in I am relieved of my childcare duties by my own mother.

After a two-week spell of picnics, digging in the vegetable patch, and eating sorbet in beds of daisies, it has started to rain.

I lie in bed and listen. Great thunderous showers.

There's a global pandemic and we are under national lockdown. We haven't been home in weeks. The media is frantic with the possibility that we won't all be on the beaches by summer.

I open the window and stick my head out. Each drop hits my face with a slight sting. I smile involuntarily.

Downstairs, I watch hailstones and droplets bounce off the pavement. The newly opened leaves on the beech tree are sagging. I can see the life coming into the garden. More every day.

I carry the baby to the door. Open it enough to let the noise in, smell the spores releasing from the soil. Wet earth. I want to show him, look.

The baby watches the drops. Eyes huge. Soft blinks taking in this world of ours.

-9

When I press on the fat in my stomach it won't go down. I am swollen, salt soaked.

All day I get bursts of rage. A leaking tap. An unwanted text. A stubbed toe. They all render me incandescent with fury. How very dare the world shift in its million little ways.

The puppy bites my toe and I bend down to unclench her jaw. Her teeth are sharp so that her mother would feel the pain and teach her not to bite. When I bend, my stomach folds on itself and I throw up in my mouth. A pocket of acid.

Last month, on the day she arrived, I cried and told her I hated her. The whimpering creature who missed her mother. I cried more, gave her an extra meal, rubbed her belly, and told her that I didn't mean it, that hormones do funny things to a person. She licked my face. I imagine it tasted salty. All day I kept a worry under my tongue, that I wanted to send her back, that we'd made a mistake. I wondered if my parents had felt this way when I was born.

The aches run up my thighs. Splitting veins and softening muscles. Familiar tides.

I sit by the fire and wait for the inevitable to cleave, fall from me, know that I will feel myself again soon.

+8

My natural pace of work is fits and starts. Project to project. Seventy hours one week, ten the next.

By work, I mean writing. Writing, reading, researching, drafting. The work I've given myself.

Being a parent, having a child, being the primary carer of a very young human, is a full-time job. Literally. In the working world, forty hours a week is considered full-time. With a child, it's every moment of every day. The full length and breadth of time. Whether you're awake or asleep. If you need a break, someone has to cover you.

Perhaps this is obvious.

At home, the house I share with the baby and his father, I can't work. Every spare resource is in use. The baby spends almost all of the time with me. When he has the baby, I am cleaning, cooking, showering, possibly eating. When he doesn't have the baby, he is cleaning, buying groceries, sleeping, and trying to keep a handle on his own mental health. We also fit in seeing family, working, and miscellaneous nonsense (filling photo albums, Christmas shopping, returning emails that fall into neither work nor socialising).

There is no time for writing.

For many years I have wanted two things: to write books and raise a family. I never considered these things to be incompatible.

The kitchen floor grows a layer of grime. Cobwebs gather behind the furniture. I clean the counters. Dust. The baby isn't sleeping. I'm not sleeping. We're running out of hours.

My house is never sparkling like my mother's. The house I grew up in, where, if there's mess, I don't see it.

Kate Zambreno says in *Book of Mutter* that, *To be a housewife, in the old mold, was to live by the rule of erasure. One's day operating around pretending that nothing occurred, no mark was made. Ordering one's life by rooms.*

The work that no one paid her for, the work I didn't notice.

•

The months bring a sliding scale, then a sharp drop. Everything awash with a negative spin, the possibility of change seems inconceivable. I have no energy and my head fills with invasive, unsettling images.

I am familiar with these symptoms. Yet they are alien to me, every time.

•

I travel to my parents' house. Home home. To rest. To work. To struggle out of myself.

•

My son and I are in my parents' house. I, the infinite child. Him, oblivious, happy.

This time I need to reset to who I am. Countryside, quiet.

In my parents' house I read. This house where I retreat to, again and again. My checkpoint. In video games there is a point where a player may restart from if their character dies or fails.

When I met the baby's father I was living with my parents by choice. After years of living in Dublin, I'd moved to their house in rural Mayo so that I could write. Living in the city working to pay rent to live in the city to work to pay rent to live in the city.

A choice between time and money. I needed to not need money. I needed time. Back in my childhood bedroom I wrote, slept, recovered from a year of heavy drinking. It was the second time since moving out at eighteen that I had moved back in. The first being when I was nineteen and had suffered a particularly acute period of anxiety and depression. I came home to recover. At twenty-four, the only thing I was recovering from was employment, exasperation, an amicable break-up. I was reeling from the city.

Now, a third time back. Back in the country.

I explained to the therapist that I had figured out how to get rid of the bad thoughts. I skipped them. Like a song on a record. I let my mind spin fast, out of focus, then fell back into the right groove.

When the thoughts I didn't want arrived, I just skipped them.

She said that was clever. I was young and cocky enough to believe she meant it, smug that I had conquered mental illness.

Is it a thought, though, or a feeling? she asked.

I could keep skipping the unwelcome thoughts. Keep distracting myself. I wouldn't have to feel anything.

•

I theorise: Part of the reason I had difficulty getting any sort of diagnosis, or treatment, was that from the outside I seemed to be doing quite well. By well I mean I was, relatively speaking, successful. I achieved the socially expected goals.

A counsellor asked me once what exactly my goal was. She was confused. Why wasn't I happy with all that I had?

I did well in school. I got into a good college. I had loving (at times) relationships. I paid my rent. I got drunk, but socially, which is so common in Ireland it was rarely factored in. I chose a career and ticked away slowly in the right direction.

I want to be happy in myself, I told the counsellor. She frowned and I knew I was asking her to perform magic.

•

If a mother is functioning well enough to mind her baby, she's probably fine.

If someone else is stepping in to get the job done, isn't she lucky to have help, she'll be grand.

+20

I'm waiting for an appointment, or perhaps to collect a prescription. Perhaps I'm still bleeding. I am washing my hands.

The poster has the same benign teal banner that sinks my stomach. It says something similar to the leaflet that I still haven't thrown away.

·

I ask Mamó about postnatal depression. It was presented then, not unlike now, as a kind of lottery.

Warned about as something you had no say over. As something that happened a couple of weeks after having a baby, being down in themselves. But you'd come up again.

If you were lucky, the granny and the likes who came in and ran the house.

She emphasises, *If you were lucky.*

An awful lot just got on with it.

If you couldn't get on with it?

I knew of some women who had to go to hospital and didn't come back for years.

Trouble having a baby. 'Ah well, there was a turn in that family'.

One woman, she tells me, who had three children, was in and out of hospital repeatedly.

The Big House, or simply Ballinasloe, were colloquial terms for the Connacht Asylum. *The local mental home.*

I think of the hotel on the hill where we had swimming classes. How many mothers went there, to hold themselves together?

I can't help wondering who minded the children then, when the mothers fell to enough pieces to be swept away.

•

I find the leaflet with the things I have not thrown away. The things I won't throw away.

I don't remember reading the leaflet. I know I did, I remember rolling my eyes at the faint hint of sunlight coming from behind a heavy blue cloud.

The symptoms seem laughably obvious now:

Irritability, anxiety, panic attacks, sleep problems, tiredness, concentration, appetite, tearfulness, obsessive behaviour.

It's not like I didn't know, at various points, on different levels.

Causes:

Personal history, birth experience, biological factors, changes in lifestyle, relationships, stressful life events, images of motherhood.

How to help yourself:

Be open, believe you'll get better, eat well, take every opportunity to rest, ask people to help you with housework, find time for fun.

Oh yes, now I remember reading it.

+2

Mothers keep telling me, *Enjoy these moments.*

Being still in myself isn't something I excel at.

In my teens, when I said,

It's not that I like being drunk, I just really don't like being sober.

I meant it as a joke.

What I meant, I think, was I didn't feel right in myself.
At least not in company.

In college, at dinner parties or open mic nights, I was
jittery, exhausted, bored. Drinking dulled the edges enough
to highlight the joy.

I never drank alone. Alone, I could lose myself in books,
reading, writing. Writing put a shape on the thoughts I
could not still.

•

With a baby you're never alone,
    always alone.

+1

It's hot in a way that feels like the world is ending.

My skin is itchy and salty. When the morphine wore off, I itched like something was alive under my skin.

The body likes to remind me that I'm an animal. The delicate systems that keep me moving, so easily thrown off. Memory, barely there. Pain robbing me of my convictions. Milk, sweat, blood, tears. Need for water.

I worry love is just an instinct.

·

Pregnant, I am told again and again that I won't write when the baby comes.

I bring a notebook to the hospital, trying to get my life's work done before my life changes. I'm worried my perspective will change so much that I'll lose everything I've been trying to say.

·

The baby comes.

I keep a notebook on the windowsill in the nursery. Wait for poems to come. They don't.

This time will pass, I'm told. I don't believe them. *Enjoy it before it's over!*

I will, I think, as long as I can write.

Is writing my ultimate immersion? Or my ultimate distraction?

•

This has happened before. Nothing here is new.

My adolescence brimmed with potential. Gone, the long, immersive presence of childhood. To come, the great adventures and freedom of adulthood.

My real life would start in college, I was sure. My days would take on the shimmer of fantasy.

•

Babies have milestones they are supposed to reach.

My milestone moments paralyse me. Every birthday an assessment.

Is this where you thought you would BE?

It is too much to be alive, not just in the moment, but to acknowledge that these days and months make up my life.

•

In the space of a day a wedding dress goes from mind's eye to attic.

How quickly potential turns to memory, or worse, regret.

The house is full of cards congratulating us.

New Home

Newlyweds

New Baby

You must be SO happy, people say. *You deserve it*, others say. It is clear that I have achieved some sort of goal, a reward for all my hard work.

Like college, I worked hard, I got lucky, I got there. *You must be so happy.*

This is your life now. You are living. Be aware of your presence in this moment, this life, this world.

(I can't.)

•

I imagined a different future. I have lived in a parallel world.

Not better, every circumstance may be the same, but life can't reflect an imagined world. My fear of this time is the same fear that brought me to reading, to writing. A deep aversion to the present. If I am living in this moment, I must be happy, I must face my mortality.

. . . I wrote so I could say I was truly paying attention. Experience in itself wasn't enough. The diary was my defense against waking up at the end of my life and realizing I'd missed it. – **Sarah Manguso**

I distract myself with the promise of a better future (self), and reflections on an imagined past (self).

Living in a dream of the future is considered a character flaw. Living in the past, bathed in nostalgia, is also considered a character flaw. Living in the present moment is hailed as spiritually admirable, but truly ignoring the lessons of history or failing to plan for tomorrow are considered character flaws. – **Sarah Manguso**

Sometimes my distractions turn against me.

•

It's hot in a way that feels like I am dying. Like we might all be dying.

I look into the future. It's like the Busted song but less quirky. This world where my son is thirty and flooding ravages the countryside.

All the futures I imagined that never came to pass.

Where the man I loved at the time died, a different monstrous fate each night. Where I was orphaned.

I rehearsed these deaths, as if imagining the pain would prevent it. Until the pain became a kind of death all of its own.

Those days I didn't live, even though no one I loved was dying.

•

Now that this is life, I must do what a mother does. I must preserve it. I am not just creator of new life, I am saver of life. I battle death daily.

Viruses, sharp corners, too warm rooms, talc, mould, blind cords, the future, petrol fumes, maniacs, a barely conscious mother.

I hobble around Dunnes, picking out frames, photo albums. In the spare minutes that I should be cleaning or sleeping, I print photographs. Like I'm trying to layer the life lived over the life living.

The first five weeks of the baby's life takes up a thick volume. I need to buy more. I try to bulk order albums online. Will we have enough shelves, to house our memories? How many days will I need to put aside to look over this reproduced life?

All my childhood, photo albums. My grandmother's walls covered in images of her six daughters, their children.

Mother is the keeper of the memories, keeper of family history. The man preserves through his name, man's language. The mothers in my family are keepers, hoarders, of memories.

Now I document the baby's every new expression in case I miss it. It takes the pressure off.

[Record freeze preserve.]

Fighting death by reproducing our days. Fighting death by reproducing. Here: your life on paper. Here: their life to come.

Sin

My secular upbringing was somewhat tainted by the religious schools my parents had no choice but to send me to.

We are born innocent and acquire sin through human corruption.

I know it like those a few years younger than me automatically know their Hogwarts house.

Something I know, intellectually speaking, is untrue, a fiction, made from a combination of myth, history, and corruption. But something that lives inside of me anyway.

The baby is born perfect. I am afraid of corrupting him.

Sustainability

I think about buying a plot of land, learning to grow vegetables. I talk about selling the house we are still unpacking
into. I need green, I need earth. The baby needs it!

We can exist in a vacuum if I work hard enough.

Self

The baby outgrows his first outfits. The newborn ones that swamped him. I keep them. I keep a memory box containing hospital bracelet, name stickers, pacifiers, wool hat. I keep the leaflets the midwives gave me on vaccines and cot death and bloodspot screening and vitamin D and breastfeeding and postnatal depression and hearing tests and public health nurse visits. I keep the photographs, even the ones I look bad in, which is all of them, but it's okay, I don't see myself anymore.

I won't throw these things away in case I throw away the wrong things. Disposing of anything associated with the baby feels sinful.

I do this. Have done this. Hoard and obsess over details. Tweaks and shuffles. Eventually, I throw it all away (the book, the man, the city, the persistence) and start again, sure this time will be different.

I'm convinced I've done it wrong. Whatever *it* is. I'm a mistake maker, an obsessive regretter.

It's control again.

Based on the flawed belief in a solid, some way superior, self. That I must be one thing, consistently; that I would reach a peak version of myself.

That I can exist in isolation. I am only a woman because there are men. I am only Irish because countries are defined. I am only a writer because people read.

We're obsessed with definitions, categories. Language, our uniquely (?) human tool.

I've married myself to a misguided focus on individuality. Is this the boring neurosis of the precocious child as an adult? I could blame being an only child, but that's too easy. I'll blame the accident of time. There's a cult of the individual in the twenty-first century. We have moved from communities, from family, towards the personal brand. Sure, we define ourselves by the groups we belong to, nationalism, gender, political parties, but it is the *I* now more than ever that holds our focus.

•

Winnicott's idea of the true and false self:

A true self based on spontaneity, instinct, desire.

The lesser, superficial self, rooted in our perception of other people's expectations.

•

The quote on the social media page as teenagers.

Be Yourself. Everyone Else is Already Taken.

Oh, fuck off, Wilde.

•

As if it were possible to live spontaneously in a world where everyone (and no one) is watching.

•

I've been thinking with my guts since I was fourteen years old, and frankly speaking, between you and me, I have come to the conclusion that my guts have shit for brains.
  – Nick Hornby, *High Fidelity*

•

The woman has lost her village. The industrial revolution changed the shape of family. Men went out to work, and the stay-at-home mum was born.

In isolation, we are easier to monetise, to capitalise.

The *Scooby-Doo* reveal meme of Fred whipping off the ghost's mask.

Is it always capitalism? Colonialism? Patriarchy?

It's always about power.

The woman is a brand now.

•

My fear that what I should be does not align with what I am stumbles when it comes to the realisation that *I* might not actually be anything specific. That *I* might not be at all.

•

I've always felt a little like I'm impersonating a human. That I might not be real.

238

Paediatrician and psychoanalyst D. W. Winnicott supposed that the false self was rooted in 'good enough' parenting in early infancy. The absence of good enough parenting left the infant wanting. A false self would be constructed by the infant to meet the mother's expectations.

Winnicott's true self was rooted in spontaneity, what we really *want*. Desire? Preverbal animal wants.

•

All my life, I've been taught to ignore my desires. This is a woman's lot.

•

My instincts tell me everyone is in danger. Standing on a rooftop, I'm afraid I'll jump, even though I know I don't want to.

•

The false self alters itself to meet the expectation of others. The mother, a stand-in for all humanity, takes the rap.

As if living in the world does not involve bending your desires to other people. As if animals don't do the same.

•

I refuse to blame my mother for the imperfections of being human.

·

I will learn to enjoy the art of the construct.

·

A human, a woman, a writer, a mother. I will cling to my identifiers, mould them because the mirror frightens me. What do they matter, anyway?

·

Before the baby, I was a writer, a student, a lover, a city girl. Stripped of my identifiers, there wasn't much left.

·

But I *am* a mother. This word and all its connotations. What do they matter?

(Nothing! (m)other needn't be biological/female. (m)other is the answer to a call no one else can hear.)

What I mean is: the baby cries and I lactate. He doesn't care about my identity crisis.

Right now, I am the world.

+7

A word so frequently come across I never questioned its meaning. I always thought of trauma as belonging to the head. A body's pain played out on the mind. Trauma was for victims of abuse, war veterans, those who were in horrific car accidents.

Cause (body). Effect (mind).

I'm slowly unknotting my binary understanding of the world, of myself. Questioning outside the lines.

In *The Body Keeps the Score*, psychiatrist Bessel van der Kolk looks at how traumatic experiences affect a person, particularly in the body's reaction, not just at the time of an event, but often years later.

Fear written into your skin. Reacting to something happening far away, long ago.

•

If I'd been traumatised, surely I would know?

Nothing really happened. Trauma refers to our response, not the event. For an experience to be traumatic all it has to do is traumatise a person.

•

Trauma, by definition, is unbearable and intolerable.

When you are forced to bear the unbearable. How does the ~~body~~ person react?

·

Van der Kolk explains that the fight / flight response exists to prompt us to escape danger. Effective action, through fleeing or fighting off the threat, ends the body's panic response. But if this response cannot be carried out, because the person is being physically restrained / there is nowhere to escape to, then, *The brain keeps secreting stress chemicals, and the brain's electrical circuits continue to fire in vain.*

In PTSD patients the body's stress hormones don't return to baseline after the threat has passed. Van der Kolk says, *The effects of trauma are not necessarily different from—and can overlap with—the effects of physical lesions like strokes. All trauma is preverbal.*

(My language, stolen from me!)

According to van der Kolk, *Trauma is not just an event that took place sometime in the past; it is also the imprint left by that experience on mind, brain, and body.* Trauma causes an actual physical change within the brain. This is what people mean when they talk about emotional scars. Bruises fade, some scars last for ever, all those clichés. This is not a metaphor. There's no room for poetry.

·

Van der Kolk explains that ordinarily the prefrontal cortex allows us to observe a potential danger, make predictions on the outcome, and make a conscious choice as to our reaction. But trauma breaks down this system, and *We become like conditioned animals: The moment we detect danger we automatically go into fight-or-flight mode.*

My assurance to myself, that I will be prepared, next time. I will anticipate everything that can go wrong. (I've done it before.)

•

Traumatised people live in a world of threat. A body braced for danger.

The new mother sees danger everywhere. It is her job.

This is my job: to predict the unpredictable. This is how I keep my baby safe.

•

In response to the trauma itself, and in coping with the dread that persisted long afterward, [severe PTSD patients] had learned to shut down the brain areas that transmit the visceral feelings and emotions that accompany and define terror. Yet in everyday life, those same brain areas are responsible for registering the entire range of emotions and sensations that form the foundation of our self-awareness, our sense of who we are. What we witnessed here was a tragic adaptation: In an effort to shut off terrifying sensations, they also deadened their capacity to feel fully alive.

•

This beautiful baby. This incomprehensible darling.

How can I love my child as much as he deserves while living in constant fear of losing him?

A call I've made before, to be numb.

(Winnicott's selves again. Maybe the false self arrives to save the true self from the pain of being alive. The feeling and unfeeling selves.)

I thumb the blister packet of the SSRIs I've used for almost a decade.

Are my sanded down edges keeping me from him, from who I could be?

I think about the years of self-medicating. The blackouts to emotionally reset. A binge, a purge. Reborn.

I told myself the absence of feeling was the same as being better.

I lived intentionally numb for a long time. It was the opposite of my coping mechanism, which had been to predict worst case scenarios. To feel it all, so that nothing could catch me unawares.

Living in this state of readiness, of perpetual grief.

Is it possible to traumatise yourself? Can fear itself become the thing we want to avoid? The body fighting off its own misjudged reaction?

Maybe the lines aren't so clear.

The body remembers. Even when we try to forget.

10 things to know about perinatal mental health

1. *You can still be a great mother even if you are experiencing perinatal mental illness.*

2. *10–15% of women can experience mild to moderate post-natal depression, fathers and partners can suffer with perinatal mental illness too.*

3. *You won't have your baby taken away if you ask for help with your mental health.*

4. *Suicide is one of the leading causes of maternal deaths.*

5. *Antenatal mental illness (untreated) is a strong risk factor for postnatal illness, so it's important to seek help while you are pregnant.*

6. *70–100% of women experience unwanted, intrusive thoughts about their baby.*

7. *Your GP or perinatal mental health team are there to discuss medication options if required, you can take most mental health medications while you are pregnant and breastfeeding.*

8. *Post-traumatic Stress Disorder is estimated to occur in 6% of maternities following an emergency section.*

9. *Women are routinely asked about their mental health at booking clinics in maternity units / hospitals.*

10. *Mental Health Midwives and Perinatal Mental Health teams provide specialist support for women.*

Outside, snow has fallen.

The light in the nursery is a brilliant grey. The baby's brow furrows at the unfamiliar. He keeps his face close to mine.

I rock. He drinks. I shush. His eyes go out of focus and flicker closed. The mechanics of naptime.

If I could lay him down during naps, then maybe I would clean the house, fold the clothes, cook something. He's almost seven months, I can't keep rocking him to sleep, when there's so much work to be done.

If I lay him on the cot, he might wake. It would throw the whole day off balance.

Besides, I don't want to.

The curve of the baby's sleeping head fits the slope of my neck. I rock.

Outside, snow has started to fall again. The flakes are big and pillowy. Part of their beauty is how soft they look, but I know if I held one for even a second it would dissolve.

I rock. I look at my phone. Scroll scroll scroll. The world is out there without me. I feel safer here, in our bunker.

The baby's breathing changes. Awake, he isn't fussing. I look down. He blinks slowly, watching out the window. He lifts his head and leans forward. Wonder rounds his mouth. Reflected in his eyes I can see the snow fall.

+7

I stand in front of the mirror with my new body. Grown and shrunk and distorted over sixteen months.

My right breast drips. Comical. A leaky tap. I watch the drops fall.

One, two, three,
Four
Five
Six
Seven.

My mother calls from outside. The baby is looking for me. To be slow is a luxury.

Stolen hours

In *Book of Mutter*, Kate Zambreno describes her dying mother, losing her mind, yelling at her family:

I have been your slave!

I think of these borrowed hours. My child on my mother's hip. These stolen hours.

Every word written while the baby is asleep. These precious minutes of mine. Or they are stolen.

In the past, in the depths of new work, I resent stopping to cook, to eat, to shower. I want to abandon my body entirely and fall down the rabbit hole of a white page, digital ink.

All the hours it has taken to get me here. Meals cooked clothes washed miles driven not to mention money earned money spent hair brushed, bathed, nappies, bicycles, late night phone calls to check I've gotten home safe. All these stolen hours.

I need you to mind the baby while I—

These hours stolen from my mother.

These hours stolen from my child

While the baby sleeps, I write.

While I write, I am not:

Cooking healthy meals.

Cleaning the bathroom.

Reading a book on Montessori and child development.

Making friends with other mums so my child will have friends.

•

In *Little Labours*, Rivka Galchen talks about the memoirs of children of writers.

> *There is a certain consistency of complaint, I have noticed, among these memoirs: the child comes to show something to the writer-parent, who is writing in a room at home during the daytime hours, and the writer-parent says to the child, I can't right now, I'm working.*
>
> *Apparently, it is very troubling for children to see their parents working, at least doing the kind of work that does not make itself visibly obvious, even if the total hours of work, and thus parental unavailability, are equal (or more likely substantially less) than the working hours of a parent simply leaving the house, to go, say, to an office, where the equally mysterious work of 'office work' is, in the child's imagination, if they are interested in the imagining, done.*

What is added to this when the writer is the mother? The background constant. It's normal for a father to go out to work each day, to be casually present. Does the everyday neglect of work hurt more from a mother?

•

I tell myself he'd rather a happy mother. Wouldn't I? Stealing all these hours that were never mine.

There are times that I am unwell. *I can't, I can't mind him.*
If she wasn't there, helping, would I try harder?

Sometimes I think I make myself sick. If I'm sick, she'll mind me. She'll mind the baby. The baby will be safe then.

•

Every word written every hour caught up on sleep every beans on toast for dinner night and haven't cleaned the house day and think I might run away day. I think how, how did she do it? How dare I make her do it all again?

•

Kate Zambreno says, *All my childhood I remember my mother cleaning.* Her mother who went mad at the end of her life. All the hours given to a family, stolen from the self.

•

I take on jobs that don't pay well. I receive an arts council grant for a collaborative project, and I edit an anthology. A friend with children asks:

How do you do it?

She knows how few hours there are. She knows the math of motherhood.

It's the meals cooked, the phone calls answered, the lifts

to doctor appointments, the afternoons and mornings and weekends. My mother's hours.

These hours that I steal.

Sometimes thoughts arrive as if from somewhere entirely alien. They buzz into my head like a bluebottle and bounce around so that I can't think of anything else. Most often, they're an image. Years ago, they were violent, unwanted images: a car crash, sex with someone I'm not attracted to, cutting my own neck.

Now, I recognise their unhelpfulness. I open the window and give the fly the choice between that or a rolled-up magazine.

I am pregnant. I have had this thought dozens of times. Been convinced, taken tests, stood sideways beside a mirror like they do on TV, swearing it's a baby and not just a wine belly.

I start to understand superstition, intuition.

I am sure.

I am familiar with my paranoia, my delusions.

When the blue line appears, I am confirmed in touch with my body, a witch.

0, +1

These new days. Here, in this realm I have been before. I want to name it a place, to suggest it is something outside of myself. A world that others know.

I feel like my skin has been sanded off.

Everything is raw. Naked. The full feel of life, which is tied so helplessly to death.

I want to numb it.

(*The patient cannot tolerate the sensation.*)

·

The first time, late at night, lying in bed, not yet seeing my first decade. Thinking of the great expanse of the universe. Trying to comprehend infinity, knowing my own finite nature for the first time. Thinking of my mother. Feeling the distance between parent and child that forms as the child morphs to adult, away from baby. The impossible ache of love, realising for the first time that someday you will be separated from this person you love most.

To be human, to comprehend our existence, is what makes us both capable of and afraid of love.

It lives in me, this undercurrent.

What have I denied myself, fleeing this feeling?

When I drank I did so under the pretence of feeling. Wanting to feel fully alive. To indulge in pleasure.

My friend who did a lot of drugs in college described ecstasy as feeling more. More alive, more in love, more happiness. Like the sensors of your body are on max.

On a merry-go-round at a festival, I felt the high of pure joy that I hadn't felt since childhood.

Outside a tent, at another festival, I became inconsolable that someone I once loved would not see the full moon again.

Both memories are hazy. Seen through a veil.

·

I am a coward. I prefer the dull pain of being numb. I don't prefer it, but I am less afraid of it.

The patient cannot tolerate the sensation.

When it came to it. I inhaled for oblivion.

Those first hours, lost to my aversion to pain.

·

Eyes so big, so black, that the whole universe looks back at me.

·

Those first hours, I have been reminded constantly, where the bond happens.

254

On the operating table. The operating table I did not plan to be on.

Distinct feeling of hands, a new part of myself.

I cling to it, the possibility of skin to skin. I ask for more pain relief.

You can't feel that.

Fiddling, pulling, I can count the surgeon's fingers. Above all, blinding pain.

Can you feel that? You can't feel that.

I think I nod.

Can you feel that?

I try to refuse the mask. I cling to it, consciousness, long enough to have the baby's face pressed to mine. I gasp for the anaesthetic.

•

This terrifying love. I have to feel it.

+8

Flicking through old photos I find selfies. Over seven or so years between the rise of the camera phone and meeting the baby's father I must have taken hundreds with the intent of impressing various men.

Head tilt lip pout that curl of hair that frames my face.

In my early twenties I used a dating app. This was how everyone I knew met romantic partners. It's how we met, the baby's father and I. Before the baby, we had no mutual connections. If things hadn't worked out then, we could have deleted each other from our lives relatively hassle free.

Is that what attracted me to the apps in the first place? Instant gratification, minimal consequences.

Pose swipe click. Pint laugh fuck. Repeat.

Your eyes.

Show me a man who hasn't used that one. Show me a woman who hasn't fallen for it.

·

Pregnant, I stop taking selfies. I don't use social media anymore. I don't want the baby to be on the internet before he's in the world.

People I know, or used to know, don't know I have had a baby. They didn't see it on social media. Social media lets you peer in on the lives of people you barely see often enough to call friends. Monumental life events occur and we celebrate together, online.

> *Needing to have reality confirmed and experience enhanced by photographs is an aesthetic consumerism to which everyone is now addicted.* – **Susan Sontag**

Now, it's not enough to take the photograph, the photograph must be posted online. Or else, did it happen at all?

•

When the baby is small, I take hundreds of selfies. Only, now I am background. Photos I send my mother or friends, the baby curled on my chest, my face bare, skin dry, eyes tired.

Your EYES.

His EYES, people often say to me. It's true, his eyes are exceptionally beautiful.

•

Here, in my parents' house, I wander back to social media. I have time, and sleeping in my old bed makes me fall into my old skin.

I'm to teach a workshop online and have to record myself. The teaching quality is poor as I'm distracted by my own image. This webcam has only previously been used for seductive purposes. My face doesn't look the same now.

•

I put on make-up and go out for a walk. I take a photo of myself in the golden light of a late spring evening. It's like looking at a photograph of someone I used to know.

•

I record a video of myself reading a poem and post it on a poetry group. Many friends 'like' it. One friend messages me to tell me I look pretty. It's been months since I've seen these people face to face. We're a week into what will become known as the first lockdown. Their isolation is new, but I've been here. *Welcome*, I feel like saying.

•

A man I barely know posts a selfie on Instagram. He reminds me of someone I used to be wildly attracted to. I click like without thinking.

I find myself posting a selfie. Filtered, hair brushed, no baby in sight. I look young. I am young, I remind myself, just not as young as I was. Likes pour in. All women now. All friends.

•

In every tired selfie I send the baby's father when we're apart he replies that I am beautiful. Even when I know I look like shit. Love, huh.

•

The possibility of posting a selfie on Instagram gets me to put on make-up, to dress nicely. I feel a little better. Less like there's concrete in my throat.

There's a small and vocal part of me that wants someone to like the signified. Want me selfishly. Don't love me.

•

The reliable 'likes' of men who you know want to fuck you. The unexpected disappointment when those disappear completely.

•

In an episode of *Scrubs* the protagonist JD, played by Zach Braff, discovers that women he thinks have disappeared have actually just gotten married.

•

Should I pretend not to know I've sold books, gotten opportunities, because my headshot makes me look prettier than I am?

•

I hated being young. I just wanted to be taken seriously.

At a literary festival several years ago, I sat in the smoking area with a group of older literati types. Several men and two women. The men mocked a female contemporary of theirs (who was not present) for being 'dramatic'. I didn't laugh, but I also didn't say anything. Neither did the two women.

•

Postnatal depression doesn't feel the same as everyday depression. Not for me, anyway. It feels like I've been inverted. Like I'm trying not to disappear.

•

I always assumed being a mother and wife would mean I'd no longer mind if I was physically attractive. I'd never considered myself vain. Though, really, anyone who writes poetry is at least a little vain.

•

Yo momma jokes don't seem funny anymore.

•

MILF.
    Just like that, I'm a porn category.

I'm afraid no one will listen to me anymore. I'm afraid to think about why they might have in the first place.

•

Fucking the man I used to be wildly attracted to was akin to putting cigarettes out on my arm. Close your eyes and tell me I'm beautiful. Shhh now.

•

In a picture of the baby's father and I, we look old and tired. We are twenty-seven and thirty-one. My dad says, *You'll look back on that and think, 'How young we looked!'* I hope we look back and think, *How sick we looked! I'm glad we got better.*

•

I think, if I get pregnant again, I'm going to take a selfie every day of my pregnancy, and every day of the first nine months of the baby's life.

Is this not what I am doing, now? Recording. Recording. Please believe I was here. Please believe I mattered.

+2

I sing to the baby. I thought that I would sing 'Greensleeves', or something memorable. I imagined myself wearing white lace.

The week before the baby was born was hot. I lay on the roof wearing sunglasses and reading. I listened to music on my phone, not consistently (I prefer silence to music as a general rule), but as songs popped into my head.

One song I played repeatedly. It had been in a TV show a decade before and for some reason kept residence in my head and occasionally popped up to say hello. I rested my phone on my huge stomach, let the white sun dizzy my vision. At different parts of the song the baby rolled and kicked.

I sing the song again, not intentionally, but it's in my head and I know the words. He smiles. On purpose! He hasn't done that before.

He kicks. I laugh.

The song I play for him has the lyric *I was born to love you*.

That lyric is the name of several other songs. Other lines of this song have been used for titles for songs too. Not intentionally, I don't suppose, but the sentiments of love, being imprisoned by love, being a part of someone else, are common choices for pop music. They all seem to be about romantic love.

The baby's favourite part is when I sing *do do do do do do do* and make a silly face. He kicks and kicks. Together we dance.

Fall

When I fell pregnant, I wasn't married.

I fell pregnant. This term is yet another thing that I've never questioned.

As if I slipped, and just:

Oops.

Pregnant.

An outdated phrase, with its implication of immaculate conception. A complete lack of male responsibility.

No one uses it anymore, really. Yet it keeps coming to me.

A fall is an accident. An intentional fall is a jump, a dive.

Fall does not convey the intent, the hope, the uncertainty.

But pregnancy *does* feel like falling. Like time turned from water – something to wade and flow through, that keeps you afloat – to air.

•

My body shirked pregnancy for a decade. A balance of flesh and hormones that was a little off. Without the regulatory effect of the contraceptive pill, I was plagued by the uncertainty of my menstrual cycle. Doctors shrugged. *It will improve when you get older*, they told me.

The absence of my period was both convenient and a worry. I took pregnancy tests knowing the likelihood was low. I couldn't trust my body. The tests were always negative.

For years, I didn't want to get pregnant. But I knew that I wanted children at some point. Yet, if I understood my body, I was only ovulating twice or three times a year. I kept using contraceptives, knowing that one day I might well be cursing every wasted egg.

·

In childhood, knowledge around menstruation was social currency. When I was nine or so, my primary school teacher, a man in his forties, told us babies came from under cabbage patches. I disagreed, and he told me to go home and ask my parents. He wasn't prepared the following day when I stood up, and recited, with great authority, an explanation that included the words penis and sperm.

·

In the hospital, I called myself *a young mother*. I was the first of my peers to get pregnant, or at least to stay pregnant with the express aim of having a baby. The consultant asked my age, then laughed and replied:

That's not young! That's not old, but it's certainly not young.

What I meant was young for this day and age, young for my socio-economic profile, young for my professional expectations. The body doesn't care.

·

I say I knew I wanted children, but I don't remember ever deciding that. It just seemed like an intrinsic part of life. I had no urge to rock a baby to sleep or get down on the floor and play Lego. Relatives' babies were cute, but quite dull. Perhaps my assumption was purely social conditioning. But I knew I didn't want to get to an age when it was too late and look back with regret.

•

My GP warned me that the pill increased your risk of stroke. I baulked. I was fifteen, and afraid of everything.

You know what else has risks? she said. *Pregnancy!* And printed off the script.

The Ireland I came of age in was slowly shaking off the Church's yoke. You could go on the pill at fifteen and buy three thongs for a euro in Penneys. Plenty of girls my age went to mass, but they wore miniskirts and heels and shifted lads in the car park around the back.

It wasn't the same country our parents had grown up in.

Still, we knew what happened to girls who had sex, who got pregnant. We knew what people said.

In the sexually liberated utopia of noughties Connacht, my friends and I learned what our bodies were for.

Our school was one of the least religious in the area, in that both boys and girls attended. But we were still greeted by Jesus on the cross every morning, and there was a chapel. Rumour had it that the old part of the building was haunted by a nun, as if the whole country isn't haunted by nuns.

It used to be full of nuns, the school. I was unsure if they moved or died off or what. I was just glad they weren't there. Their mascot hung above the doors in most classrooms. The Virgin.

Our school stood out as progressive. The girls and boys both wore trousers! The particular stretchy material used in the girls' trousers rose to provincial fame.

The school with the asses! I was told more than once when giving the name of my school to a peer from elsewhere in the county.

I don't remember talking about our bodies with my friends growing up. Or, when we did, it was in the context of male pleasure. What would we let boys do to us.

There were contradicting expectations on teenage girls. At fifteen, the vehement denial of masturbation by every girl in our group of friends, while the boys celebrated its role in their lives. We were to not only be virginal, but to be entirely void of sexual desire.

Yet when a girl was in a relationship with a boy, their friends quickly started to ask how far they'd gone. How far? A mixed analogy presumably learned from watching *American Pie*. Shifting (kissing), handjob, fingering, blowjob. I don't remember hearing about cunnilingus in social circles until college. The ultimate act: penetrative, heterosexual sex.

The language of riding.

I love slang. Its possibilities, its poetry, its celebration of the vernacular. It betrays me with its cloaking, its exclusionary abilities.

Sexual acts occurred in an undisputed order, each some kind of reward for a boy's commitment. The girl was giving something, the boy was taking. The girl wasn't supposed to want it.

At sixteen, a female friend was criticised by her boyfriend for not making enough noise during sex. Another friend who wasn't sexually active was hounded constantly by male friends and acquaintances. They assumed that the lack of a boyfriend meant an available position, not a choice. When she rejected them, they called her a tease.

You were to be the virgin, then automatically the whore. You were to have the kind of sex seen in pornos, but deny ever feeling horny.

Fucked, whether or not you were fucked.

•

My friends who have kids are a decade or so older than I am.

The ones with babies and toddlers spent their twenties building their careers. The kids go to crèche, and the parents go back to work quickly, to pay for the mortgage, the childcare, the balance.

A few women I know who had kids in their early twenties are now in their late thirties starting careers. Their kids are grown or are in school and low maintenance. Money is a struggle.

There's some envy on both sides, and a lot of *I wouldn't swap it though*.

•

Story goes, Mary (*the* Mary) stayed a virgin. I didn't know that. I'd have thought after getting married, delivering the Lord's baby, and losing her only son to save humanity, she might at least get the ride. But nope.

•

When a teenage girl had had sex, everyone knew. It was written on the back of bus seats, the pharmacist who sold the condoms told the boyfriend's mother, the guy only told one friend who then told anyone who'd listen, some teachers overheard gossip and partook.

The language that surrounded those teenage girls.

Slut slag gagging ride whore easy bike lock want slut.

It wasn't uncommon for a teenage girl's sexuality to be the subject of wink and elbow language among parents at the school gate. The out of control girls. The girls to keep your sons away from.

You'll ruin your life getting pregnant.

The only effective birth control is abstinence.

I knew I was lucky not to be a teenage mother. I was careful, but made mistakes, yet my body didn't seem to want pregnancy. My body indulged in sin but avoided the consequences.

Abortion was illegal. Being anti-choice (at least publicly) was the norm. I knew girls who had babies at fifteen, sixteen, even eighteen. Their future always seemed to be set: live with their parents, wave goodbye to third-level education, fall away from all social circles. They weren't locked away, sent to institutions (now punishment came in the form of poverty, of lost careers, of discrimination), but the country remembered a time when they would have been, and not everyone thought times had changed for the better. The least these girls could do now was to have the decency to be ashamed.

I never heard so much as a whisper of a girl going to England for an abortion. Maybe none of them did. Maybe that was the one part of a girl's sexual health that could be kept secret.

•

My peers aren't having children. Most of the people I know live in the city. The lucky ones rent and survive month to month. When they're not working, they want to relax, go drinking, travel.

More and more of my female friends say, *I don't want kids.*

•

Maybe none of this happened this way. Maybe I was paranoid. I could still be.

•

My body didn't want to get pregnant. (*You're so lucky!*) It was convenient, but I knew it wouldn't always be. Time made me gamble.

We knew a couple going through the many heartaches of IVF. I had a friend who was a first-time dad in his forties, exhausted to the point of sickness. We didn't want to do it that way.

Marriage and babies were connected, somehow, sure? But not causally, not chronologically. Sometimes, getting married at all felt antiquated and patriarchal. I wasn't changing my name. I was obviously no virgin. Apparently, there were tax implications, but I didn't really understand them.

Yet, we were romantic.

We'll get married next summer! we said. A long engagement. A big but casual wedding. We were excited, relaxed.

Then, when a due date was given, *The summer after that!* We'd have our one-year-old at the wedding. That was the plan.

As we counted the weeks in months, the months in trimesters, that was the plan.

•

The term 'fallen women' is linked to the fall of man. Biblical, original sin, and all that. Fallen women were women who had lost their innocence. In the eighteenth century, the term was synonymous with prostitutes. The Magdalene asylums were set up in Ireland to house fallen women. Also known as the Magdalene laundries, these institutions were religious run and state supported. They functioned as commercial laundries, and the women worked, sometimes for their whole lives, as essentially slave labour.

The parameters of the definition of fallen women expanded during the nineteenth and twentieth century: women in these institutions weren't exclusively prostitutes, but women who had gotten pregnant out of wedlock, women who were known to be sexually active outside of marriage, and women who were wayward or difficult.

To be a fallen woman was to be a woman who broke the rules, and Ireland of that time had no patience for women who broke the rules.

•

The baby would have my name in the hospital, like he was more mine than his father's. Unmarried, I would be the baby's sole guardian until we applied to have this changed. I ticked the 'single' box repeatedly on forms. I felt judgement I wasn't sure was there.

These loaded words. What they carry for me. Do they carry the same for others?

I have my father's surname. In primary school my mother had a discussion with my teacher which turned heated.

Who are you to her anyway? he said. It was a school of fewer than sixty students. He'd met her several times. But we didn't share a surname.

My parents were in their early twenties when I was born. They had been a couple for five years, and, despite my grandparents' frustration, lived together most of that time. They are still together now. They never married. I found out, registering my own son's birth, that my father was never my legal guardian. In Ireland, a father is only a legal guardian if married to the mother, or if the parents apply for a court order. In the eyes of the state my mother was unmarried, and that was all that mattered.

If I had been born a generation earlier, or even just a decade earlier, under slightly different circumstances. Where would society have felt they had the right to send my mother?

•

My paternal grandfather's sister told us a story once about their mother. I was a child at the time. Eleven or so, on the brink.

My great-grandfather died when my grandfather was young, leaving my great-grandmother a working-class single mother. My great-aunt said she remembered the nuns coming to the door, knowing her mother had teenage girls. An offer to take them away. Her mother hiding the girls in a cupboard and running the nuns out of the house.

•

When again would it be just us, to celebrate just us? Why should we wait? I didn't want to be judged for getting married while pregnant, but if we were so liberated, why should that stop us? We applied for a marriage licence, just in case. There was romance to it.

Yet I knew I had conservative reasons too. A whisper in the back of my head that I couldn't shake.

I disgusted myself. Family unit? These terms of conservative rhetoric used in the referendum on same-sex marriage: *A baby needs a mother and a father.*

It's not just eye-rollingly conservative. (*Man woman marriage baby.*) This way of thinking is insidious. It is used to maintain a patriarchal power structure. To create an Other of lone parents, LGBTQ+ parents.

A family unit? The presenting of the nuclear heterosexual family as the ideal. Some divine design, not an evolving display of human relationships and affections.

I grew up in a secure family. I never doubted my parents' relationship or their love for me. They weren't married.

A family can be a mother, father, child. It can be a single parent and child. It can be a child and their legal guardians. It can be a couple and their pets. It can be a person and their friends. It is what you make it, as long as there's love, you'll be okay.

I knew all of this.

Yet there was shame revealing itself in my body. It had been dormant. I felt like I was fifteen, afraid of being pregnant, of being exposed as something sinful. Decades after the shame was supposed to have lifted.

•

Ireland has a history of institutions. A systemic dependence. The last Magdalene laundry closed in 1996. I was three. The last mother and baby home closed in 1998.

Mother and baby homes: religious run institutions that took women carrying 'illegitimate' babies and housed them until their babies were born. The women worked, sometimes for a year or more after their child was born, to pay for their and their baby's upkeep. Some women were moved to the laundries, some went home. Thousands of babies were adopted. Those that weren't stayed in the homes until aged three before being moved to industrial schools. Sometimes girls from the industrial schools would move on to the laundries, their whole lives in one institution or another.

I think of one of Mamó's sayings:

But for the grace of God.

Even without her faith, I have internalised the message. It's the same thing I keep reminding myself, the luck of my circumstance.

Mamó married before she had the first of her six children. She acknowledges her fortune, wanting to get married, wanting six children. She had to give up her job in the civil service when she got married. That was the law. Sometimes, if a parent was alive or willing, they would mind a mother's children. But other than that, a mother stayed home. She didn't earn for herself.

But, she tells me, it was assumed the father would financially support you.

That wasn't always the way it happened, she says, *but that was the way it was supposed to be.*

My grandmother had had four of her children by the time the unmarried mother's allowance was introduced.

I ask her about the homes. Did people know? When she was growing up, when my mother and her sisters were?

None of us knew anything about it. We knew there was a home that a girl could go into to have a baby. But it stopped at that. We didn't realise that her baby could be taken from her.

You'd hear, such and such has gone to England. England being the euphemism for the mother and baby homes then, as it was for abortion in my adolescence. She tells me that sometimes a couple would go to England and get married once they got there, but they wouldn't risk staying in Ireland.

In later life I knew one girl, not far from us here, who was about fifteen, sixteen, went off into one of those places. Her mother was wondering where she was. Thought she had a job. She got a letter from her, and went down, hauled her out of there and brought her home.

She tells me that this girl realised there that she was considered a *fallen woman*. It's what was said, she puts on a voice to imitate the gossip:

Girls like that, no control.

My grandmother sighs.

Ireland, in its own way, was quite cruel.

•

My soon-to-be-husband made pre-emptive jokes about shotgun weddings. He tried to understand when I got cross. Sometimes a woman is tired of her body being the punchline.

We watched *The Simpsons* episode with pregnant bride Marge more than once. It cheered me up. It was my choice not to wait, after all.

•

The girl would never be back where she was in people's esteem.

'She had a baby you know. Don't let Johnny go around with her.'

•

Not sharing a name sometimes made me feel like I didn't belong to my mother. (*Who are you to her anyway?*) She was young and beautiful, and people regularly said, *No way are you her mother*, in a way that was supposed to be a compliment.

But sometimes I felt like I didn't belong to the earth, like I wasn't real. Maybe looking towards my unmarried parents is just another wish for an explanation to that feeling. I could never lose my name to marriage, there wouldn't be enough of me left. Did I think I could ground myself in names, in people?

Could I protect my child from the anxieties of existence by tying him to tradition?

•

Pregnancy made me feel guilty. A visceral response. A recurring thought when I saw someone glance at my bump: they're thinking about me having sex.

It's so embedded in my relationship to my body.

•

In the twentieth century Ireland had the highest number of patients per capita in mental hospitals in the world. The district asylums had been set up in the nineteenth century, as an antidote to the overflowing cells for lunatics in work-houses and county hospitals. Though religious orders ran laundries, industrial schools, and mother and baby homes, they were never involved in mental hospitals, which were entirely state run institutions.

Yet both have their roots in the institutions of eighteenth-century Ireland. A colonised Ireland. In 1703 the first House of Industry was established in Dublin. The workhouse was a place of asylum for the poorest of the country. The able bodied were expected to work. The inmates included paupers, lunatics, aged and infirm, abandoned children. It was a place of punishment or correction for vagabonds, sturdy beggars and disorderly women. Lunatics were bound in heavy chains. In 1805 Sir John Carr in his Tour of Ireland described the treatment of inmates in Limerick House of Industry:

A gloomy abode of mingled want, disease, vice and malady, where lunatics were loaded with heavy chains and fallen women bound and logged.

In 1727 the house was renamed the Foundling Hospital and Workhouse of Dublin City. Foundlings were babies brought anonymously to the workhouse. Foundling hospitals were intended to avoid infanticide of illegitimate children. The hospital was closed in 1835 due to high mortality rates. One of the doctors had been poisoning the babies.

The workhouses closed in 1920, abolished by the Irish Free State. But many institutions did not close, and more were to open. There still existed the need for somewhere to place the unwanted. The insane, the poor, the fallen women, the illegitimate children.

With Catholicism and Nationalism bound so closely, the shackles of one oppressor were shaken off, while welcoming another.

•

We married with the baby dancing under layers of lace and silk, skin and muscle. It wasn't just the two of us, the man who became my husband, the baby's father, the man who would, eventually, no longer be my husband. It was three of us. Love brought us there.

·

First my aunt, then my mother, had a baby in their early twenties. It was the 1990s. Both unmarried. Both still with their children's fathers over twenty years later. My cousin's parents married eventually, mine didn't.

It's surprising the number who got married afterwards, as long as no one raised an eyebrow. I wonder if my parents never did to avoid the raised eyebrows. My mother, the private person, who never wants to be centre stage. Her daughter, the opposite.

The world has changed in some ways. (So am I living in the past?)

·

My inexplicable need for my child's parents to be married. As if marriage is proof of something. Is this one step away from having him baptised 'just in case'? A gambler in the clutches of an addiction. Living the contradictions to my beliefs.

What if what if what if.

The fall through generations. The inheritance of trauma.

Ireland, in its own way, was quite cruel.

•

I don't know enough about the validity of epigenetics to theorise. But whether in our genes or through the warnings our mothers have given us, the warnings we've deduced ourselves from how men treat us, the women of Ireland hold something of the past in their bodies.

•

The year my parents met; the Status of Children Act abolished the status of illegitimacy.

•

I didn't want the baby to ever question whether or not he was wanted.

•

There's a shift, I think. A space for mothers in Ireland that didn't used to exist.

The rallying, the action, that followed the death of Savita. That led to the eighth amendment being repealed.

The outcry at the inadequacy of the Mother and Baby Home Commission.

Maybe women and mothers have always been angry. There are hints now that the country might be starting to listen.

Still, there are reasons for rage. The National Maternity Hospital being built on land owned by the Catholic Church. The prolonged restrictions in maternity units during the pandemic. Continued resistance is necessary.

•

I'm aware of the luck of timing.

During early days of my pregnancy, the news was alight with the finalising details of new abortion laws in Ireland. Nausea and panic rocked my body. Someone as many weeks pregnant as I was who wanted an abortion would have to travel outside of the state. I tracked the numbers, the weeks. Someone who fell pregnant the same night as I did who did not want to remain pregnant would be missing the legal cut-off by a week.

I was lucky. It wasn't a question for me. As my wanted pregnancy began to distort my mind and body, I kept choosing: *yes.*

+8

The documentary shows a torch underwater. The sound of breathing. It's a re-enactment. An illustration shows the bend in the route where the first diver got jammed against a rock, how his companion had no choice but to swim past his body.

The tunnel under rock, full of water. The black and on and on.

Knowing that it ends in surface breaking, air.

Because it ended last time.

Because others swam it first.

But the chance, that first, you might run out of air.

Years ago, I watched a different film about cave diving. This was before, when I thought I would be the sort of person who did things. Instead, I am the sort of person that is things. Wife, mother, writer.

The two films fall over each other like memories and a dream.

In one, the TV presenter smiles. He's English, posh. Breaking the surface at the end, his smile splits out of the mask.

You just have to keep swimming. Swimming. Know the air is coming. Know that sometimes there are bodies ahead.

–8

Marbled grey, a black fist. The screen wobbles. I know I should be seeing the unmistakable silhouette.

In the pit of the black,

a star. A white twinkle.

The sonographer says words I don't know in this context.

Foetal pole. Yolk Sac.

I know nothing in this context.

Synapses spark. A rush of thoughts.

I think of an egg, nourishment, veganism, childhood, animal.

I think of the Arctic, magnetic fields, forces I don't understand, the North Star, finding a way home.

0

To be opened up,
parts of you to be touched by air that never have been before.
Hands reach in,   tug   squeeze   cut.
I want to get away from them.
Inside my head I move like a bird against glass.
I want to kick them away, to run.

> But I can't move, and if I could my body would follow.
> My pain I can't escape.

+8

I must take a thousand photos of his sleeping face. None do it justice. Should I describe it? The plump cheeks, the dark eyelashes, the pursed lips. The soft sweep of golden hair. That could be any sleeping baby.

How to describe the awe of the most perfect face.

Again, words fail me. But that's okay.

1

My mother hangs the wedding flowers to dry. When the baby is born, a rose my grandmother bought will be blooming. My mother will save it, airlocked beneath a plastic dome, like Belle's enchanted rose. But my mother is smarter than the beast, kinder than the enchantress, she dries the flower first. It will look the same when my son is grown.

I didn't lick it off the stones, my desire to preserve.

We pressed petals between the pages of the complete works of Lewis Carroll. An old orange flower press holds decades-old daisies and bleeding hearts.

I have a bouquet of dried roses from the day I graduated from my masters. The day I found out I was pregnant. My mother saved them for me.

She presses, dries, hangs, preserves.

All the best photos of my son, she took.

A mother's work. Keeping track of it; the life so quickly passing.

Secret (+2, +4, +8, ~)

It doesn't make sense that I should be so unprepared. Only later, much later, does it occur to me that I had rehearsed many lives through literature. Vicarious adventure. But motherhood, the intricate details of the quotidian, was not a literary subject I had come across. The moral, emotional, and psychological effects of motherhood seemed rarely touched upon.

•

We whisper things in secret. Other mothers come to me; they are welcoming me into the fold. This is what women have been doing for generations, wrapping shame in our hands and slipping it to each other, like a relative giving a child a fiver without letting anyone see.

•

When I am pregnant, I agree to partake in a writers' group at the arts centre in the town near where I grew up. The project the group will work on will start when the baby is seven weeks old. Pregnant, I am imagining a world where the baby fits into my life, and quickly.

I am lucky. This is not what going back to work looks like for most new mothers. I'm on maternity leave, but it's unofficial. A writer, I hop between commissions and courses. My maternity leave is symbolic and self-inflicted. I don't intend to go 'back to work' when the baby is seven weeks old. But it's just one day a week. And, unlike so many, I love my work. Without it, I'm not sure there's much of me left.

When the project goes ahead, I worry I am boring the other writers. I am a poet, but I can't write poems. I seem only to manage bursts of words. But they're not relevant. They're all about the baby. I speak like I'm the first person to have one. I'm embarrassed. I do what I know, I write, but my writing is not the same. Even this part of myself has morphed, it's unrecognisable.

After the second week, one of the writers asks if I have read Claire Kilroy's essay on motherhood. I haven't. I haven't read anything much about motherhood, really. I go home and I find the essay. I read it over several hours, stolen minutes, on my phone while the baby sleeps.

The essay leads me to a book. I buy the book and keep it by the rocking chair. I read snatches of it, slowly, over months. The book leads me to another book, which leads me to two more.

All this time, the mothers have been talking.

•

One of the first literary works on motherhood I read is Rachel Cusk's *A Life's Work*. She says what I suspected, what I have feared, that other writers too question if writing on motherhood is only of interest to other mothers.

In the hundreds of poetry readings I have been to over the years, the audience is usually made up of at least 50 per cent poets. If writing on motherhood is only read by other mothers, it is not the first to have a seemingly small target audience. Yet poetry is lauded as a fine art with an ability to convey universal truths.

In her essay 'Maternal Landscapes' Carolina Alvarado Molk says:

There's a prevalent fear that engaging artistically with a domestic realm will be dismissed as a trivial or superficial pursuit.

Yet, the one universal, undeniable truth is that we are all born, and we all die. Why are we not more curious about the person closest to our beginnings?

This is a point made again and again by writers who happen to be mothers:

All human life on the planet is born of woman.
– **Adrienne Rich**

(And still the shock comes!)

Perhaps we don't want to look too closely at the beginning, any more than we really want to see the end.

Or perhaps acknowledging the amount of unpaid, unappreciated labour that goes into our upbringing poses too much of a problem. (I myself can only write because my own mother is caring for my son. What then is the value I am placing on her time?) That real, en masse appreciation of this fact might upset the capitalist focus of the status quo. That we may have to make room in our society for breastfeeding in public without buying a four quid coffee.

So, we dismiss it. Writing about early motherhood. As chubby babies, stinky nappies, too many adjectives. Mush.

In the heat and panic, the complete shifting of my brain, I insisted, *No one told me it would be like this.*

The dozens of articles I had read on buggies and co-sleeping, on hypnobirthing and the seventeen uses for Sudocrem. All that I hadn't read.

This conversation I had no interest in being part of. I am complicit in my ignorance. As much as anyone, I thought of poems about babies as dull, irrelevant to my own concerns.

Novels and memoirs by women writing artfully and with vulnerability about their motherhood weren't hard to find once I learned where to look . . . I'd never set out to find memoirs about motherhood before I became a mother, but neither had I stumbled across them. – **Carolina Alvarado Molk**

All the voices I'd never thought of seeking out.

Molk speaks of finding memoirs on motherhood in the parenting section, rather than with other literary memoirs. Are we surprised? Women's philosophy is self-help. Women's fiction is chick lit.

I think of all the books I've read about young men getting fucked up.

Violence. Love. Mortality. Time.

Most of the time, I don't feel real. I have learned to relate to people through pages. I feel closer to human when reading. Maybe that's the sign of a good writer, letting the reader feel like they understand you.

291

The images of common extraordinary moments the mother writes. They can't mean anything to the reader. What we, as writers, are trying to *say* is invariably not what the reader reads. What we intend to make them feel is not necessarily what they do feel.

It's like reading of the mechanics of love. Boy meets girl. The replayed narrative, a thousand times over . . .

I look for myself in these books. It's not difficult once I try. Perspectives not dissimilar to my own are available. I am white, middle class-ish, cis-gendered. I am a mother because I chose to be one.

All the conversations I had the luxury of not partaking in. I am complicit in my ignorance. I want to read the mothers that mothers like me Other. They are harder to find, I'm not looking hard enough. Like everyone, I'm too busy looking at myself, too busy not looking at myself hard enough.

I search for books by mothers. I begin to tuck away these books. Each one I read leads me to two more, like a secret code. I stay up, the baby snoring softly, clinging to my side, and read.

These books became the close friends that held these secrets and shared them. – **Carolina Alvarado Molk**

A network of women whispering across coffee tables. Shouting in text.

–5

I have to sleep on my side to be sure that the weight of my body doesn't cut off the blood flow to the baby. These tiny risks.

I keep waking on my back. I'm not used to putting restrictions on my body.

The body's self-sabotage.

+3

My parents and husband are doing some out loud calcu-
lating. It's for the cost of a buggy or an Indian takeaway
or something.

A hundred and forty three euros and fifty two cents I say,
patting the windy baby's back. They look at me like in that
scene in *Matilda* when she answers the insanely long multi-
plication question. They are Miss Honey and the
six-year-olds, aghast.

My mother says what the men haven't earned the right
to say:

*I forgot you could do that. No offence, but I forgot how stupid
pregnancy made you.*

+8

I collect my books. Stitch together conversations between these people, their overlapping ideas. My mother shelf, or stack. Not all of them are women, or mothers. But it's my mother shelf anyway. The shelf that draws me from isolation.

•

They weren't texts so much as talismans to be held against annihilation. – **Olivia Sudjic**

•

I come across the same arguments, the same images, the same despair. I reread each one, keep a stack beside my bed.

A myth: our survival depends on our unique selling points.

As if any book is written alone, any life lived alone.

•

Our capitalist world depends on novelty. Infinite growth. Our deluded narcissism. We (who?) aim to be the next big thing.

Nothing here is new.

•

The future of civilisation, and possibly the species, depends on renewable energy. Renewable, to make new again. (Impossible!) Something that can be begun again.

•

The earth doesn't need our inventions. The earth needs us to go back, to go slow. The earth doesn't need us at all, *we* need us to go back, to go slow.

+8

Sleep is medicine. Words are medicine.

+5

Let's move to Spain, I say every few months. Sitting in a bar in Vigo in 2016, I watched three couples eat tapas and drink wine, while their children played around them. It didn't have the same feeling as the kids bribed with salt and vinegar Tayto while their dad had his pint of Guinness.

When we were in Malaga, the playgrounds were full well into dusk.

My evenings are the most social part of my life. It used to be alcohol fuelled, meeting friends for drinks. But even without booze. Poetry readings, pubs, exhibitions, restaurants. I like the idea of being able to go out at night with my child, or at least not being banished from society because of him.

•

I'm asked to read a poem at the launch of a journal. The venue is five minutes' walk from our house. All plans must be made with careful consideration as to whether or not the baby will be asleep at that exact time.

I wrap him to my body with the stretchy sling. He falls asleep on the walk, the bobble from his hat bopping away in time with my steps. I make small talk with other writers. Two, with grown children, are reassuring, kind, impressed that I'm outside.

My husband and I sit in the front row. The plan is to pop the baby on his lap when it's my turn to read. But the baby is asleep, and I don't want to wake him.

If he's still asleep I'll just do the reading wearing him. He's barely noticeable.

Another reader has brought her children. They're older than mine, not babies, but not yet ten. They fidget and run up and down the stairs.

My name is called and the baby is still asleep. When I reach the mic, he stirs. Before I have my first sentence out, his head has raised and turned to the audience. We're spot-lit. I get through the poem without laughing.

We take our seat and he nurses. Afterwards, he's complimented profusely by anyone I speak to. I'm beaming.

+7

The baby likes to tangle his left hand in my hair while he feeds. He grabs the loose strands of what was my fringe, and loops them between his fingers. He pulls the hair taut and I bite my grimace away.

When he does this, cheeks pulsing with the steady suck and swallow of milk, his eyes go out of focus, lids closing. His grasp loosens. After his drink, he smacks his lips softly and rests his cheek on my chest.

I replace my hair with my little finger and lie down beside him on the mattress, my arm arched around him. He seems both bigger and smaller in the adult bed. I fall asleep, my finger still in his palm.

+8

Nothing about this is new.

I've been here before.

I reach my small epiphanies. I breathe.

I wake up. I don't sleep. My body moves, but I've been left behind.

I was okay. I was okay and now I am not.

Who says we have to start at a beginning? Who makes the rule that stops us at a destination?

Feminist('s) son

Imagining the baby as an adult, reading what I write, I worry. I worry, more than anything, about his pain. I see Rivka Galchen's image of the closed office door.

I am again projecting, imagining. I should think instead to look around, to look back.

I am not the first mother to write.

In the 1998 preface of his mother's book *With Child* Ariel Chesler reflects on having a mother as a writer. In 2018, he revises the preface for a new edition now that he too is a parent. This is the edition I find, buy online, have delivered to my house.

> *Although I found her work interesting and was proud, I was jealous of the time and attention it took away from me. I can still recall standing at her office door. It was shut, but that meant nothing to me – I was her one and only son. A mother could always be taken for granted, a mother could always be counted on, I thought to myself. I knocked calmly and entered before she could reply. Her books surrounded her as usual and she was sitting with a pen in hand. 'I'm off duty!' she informed me. I did not comprehend that phrase and replied, 'You are not a taxi, Mom. I need to talk to you.'*

As if Galchen was speaking directly about him, though I have no reason to believe that she was. Will the baby grow to call at my office, to feel abandoned? If I were a good mother, I'd throw my laptop out. I'd burn my books. I'd never read or write another word while he needed me.

What sort of feminist would that make me? What sort of mother?

Ariel's mother is the feminist writer and intellectual Phyllis Chesler. She's a radical feminist, a second wave feminist. Feminism wasn't a question for me. It's the privilege of my upbringing that being a feminist has never felt at odds with the world I live in, at least, not the world I am at home in. But this privilege has at times limited my understanding, my willingness to do my homework. I have taken liberties for granted. Feminism so often felt like a historical position rather than one of daily awareness and action.

Why would a mother not be able to write? Fathers write. Was the worst challenge for the mother writer being asked by interviewers where their children were when they wrote?

•

When my grandmother got married, she had to give up her job. It was the law. When I asked her about it, she said it was presumed that if you had children, you raised them yourself. It wasn't seen as a sacrifice to stay at home:

No, it was assumed that you'd get married and have children and raise those children yourself. Only teachers had childminders or those with involved grandparents.

In the civil service it was written in that when you got married you gave up your job.

There wasn't as much of childminding, except those lucky enough to have parents. Shopkeepers and the like had their children with them. It was coming in, the idea that a woman would feel in any way hard done by.

Later, we were in the EU, there was talk about getting 'back to work'. It was always in the background. Farmers' wives had a source of income, chickens, bainbh, and that was her money.

It was accepted that the mother would be there.

•

The second wave feminists fought for female equality. There's an image of the oppressed housewife becoming radicalised and walking out on her family.

In this way we have failed in our grasp at equality by aiming to live like A Man in a man's world. Coming of age in the early-twenty-first century, I had a naive assumption. I would go to work after college. I would have a family, because I wanted one, but, being a feminist, I would go back to work. Who would mind my children? I didn't think of it. The domestic is so rarely brought into focus.

(These are not new ideas. (Nothing here is new.))

Housewife, homemaker. They are not real jobs. They are roles of patriarchal oppression. They are not jobs, there is no *work* there.

Clean floors, change bedding, laundry laundry laundry, burp baby, change baby, feed baby, feed family, unclog drain, clean fridge, put out clean towels, hoover behind the radiator.

If there's a mountain of housework the homemaker is Sisyphus.

Why would I think of all the unseen work my mother did? My grandmothers' houses were sparkling my whole childhood.

When I found *With Child*, I didn't recognise the author's name. No doubt because I am as guilty as anyone at not being interested in books on motherhood until I found myself alone, desperate for understanding from people who came before me.

I haven't just been taking my mother for granted. I've been taking all mothers for granted.

·

Child: I'll search for Mothers, dead and alive, to guide me. In dusty manuscripts, in new anthologies, in my living room or theirs, Chesler says in the first entry of her book. She is pregnant, already a lauded feminist. She has her own struggle to battle through. A reminder that the information, the support I sought, has been sought before. This network of women across countries, across decades.

Nothing here is new. Nothing can be new.

A voice, a baby's voice, decades later.

What better birthday gift could I have received? It is a tangible, never-ending gift to celebrate my life. I feel so blessed, so lucky to have this book.

Ariel Chesler, the self-confessed radical feminist, in conversation with his mother. Ariel Chesler, who in a few pages will be a squirm beneath her skin, who will be the child who knocks on the office door of the woman who's about to write this diary.

I am not the first mother to write a book.

I wonder, sometimes, what my mother writes about me in her diary. She records too. It's something of a genetic sickness, perhaps.

We record, we want to beat it (time).

I know I'm going to make mistakes. I will set out not to make any. We all do. The child can look back, can tell the parent their mistakes, what they did right.

The new parent is a child in need of a parent, the new parent realises the parent was a child all along.

Ariel Chesler ends his preface with the end of his mother's book:

'And who could be closer than we two?' *To which I reply to her, No one mother, no one.*

I want to tell my son that this book is and isn't about him. That I write to better myself, to be a better mother. That being a happier person will make me a better mother. That I want him to grow up in a world where mothers are people. That I want him to take me for granted, to be counted on, that I won't mind when he interrupts me in my office because that's what parents are for. That I'll smile and laugh and invite him in because it's not unusual for me to be working, nor unusual for me to not be working. That if I thought it was the right thing for him, I'd choose to put it all away for ever.

+8

Surrounded by soft and sleeping creatures. Dog, cat, baby. I am tired. I come home, again and again, to my parents' house. Here, I am the me I was when I lived here, all of them. Permanently stalling myself at nine, twelve, seventeen, twenty-one. The times I lived here, with a whole vague future. The solidity of the present terrifies me. A hundred alternatives drop away. I scold myself for my ingratitude, stare harder at the baby's face. I pretend to still be young. Ask my mother's permission to drink orange juice. Parentchild. Motherbaby.

I don't know if I'm depressed or just incredibly tired.

I catch the smell of him, soft and loved, and think it is incomprehensible that this creature is of me.

But at first it didn't seem strange. Because he wasn't. Or perhaps he was, but any part of me was unrecognisable. My body and mind. Living in a new place. I couldn't put this life against the one I'd lived.

This surreal world in which a baby fed from me. In which I was a wholly new person.

+8

I sleep.

I walk the gardens I spent my childhood in, listen to the birds, the gentle munch and low of the cattle, the wind in the ash trees. I exhale and relax, little by little.

Now, when I sit down to write, the words come differently.

I overthink, too self-aware again. In my healing, something has broken.

I start thinking in full sentences and metaphors again.

My old brain is returning, to a life she doesn't know.

•

I can think, write, outside the immediate again. Just for short bursts. Long enough to read, to capture, to imagine.

Maybe my old self will return. Maybe I can take something of this newness with me.

I mustn't let myself forget how to *be*.

Extraordinary devotion

so much depends
upon
a red wheel
barrow
glazed with rain
water
beside the white
chickens

William Carlos Williams puzzling undergraduates for decades. The joke that he was so stingy with words he used the same one twice in his own name.

So much depends on it. What?

The simplicity of what is barely seen. The ordinary image, beautiful despite its mundanity.

What depends on it?! the students cry.

So much, the professor says.

They all pretend to understand.

•

One of the most influential thinkers on the subject of child psychoanalysis was the paediatrician D. W. Winnicott. Even now, fifty years after his death, I had heard of his 'good enough' mothering theory. His influence can be seen in the social media cartoons presenting ideas of attachment parenting. He was, among other things, a man, and a doctor.

In her book *Mad, Bad, and Sad: A History of Women and the Mind Doctors from 1800 to the Present*, Lisa Appignanesi says that *Winnicott made babies interesting.*

Appignanesi looks at the twentieth-century psychoanalysts in the context of the need to repopulate after the wars and the 1918 pandemic.

Undoubtedly a world war, followed within a single generation by another, fed into the process that made a healthy mother and child — the so-called nursing couple — a prime preoccupation for the mind doctors.

Winnicott's onetime supervisor, Melanie Klein, was an influential early child analyst. For Klein, the baby's feelings towards their mother needed to be met by the mother's attachment and bond. In Klein's ideas, the mother's affections, and her body (primarily the breast) are the prototypes for a child's future interpersonal relationships. Appignanesi theorises that:

In the culture at large into which Klein's complex hypotheses gradually fed in a simpler form, her sense of the mother as both utterly passive and infinitely responsible helped to induce in women a feeling of lingering culpability with regard to their children.

A lot of pressure on the mothers. Winnicott's popularity, not just among those in the field but among the everyday parent, could be down to his championing of the ordinary parent. If so much depended on those early years, how could anyone possibly get it right? For Winnicott, the mother just needed to be an:

Ordinary good mother . . . devoted to her infant.

The stairs are unhoovered. Flecks of coffee have dried into the kitchen counter. I sidestep piles of laundry in the bedroom, the bathroom. In the skylight a spider pirouettes, builds her home in ours, signalling my untidiness.

Before the baby, I wasn't all that clean or tidy. When I lived in flats in the city, I didn't see the soap scum building up in the sink, never thought of the cobwebs. Empty bottles lined the countertop like soldiers.

Now I fret about the build-up of dust. I imagine my son as an adult reflecting on his childhood as messy, neglectful.

•

One is not born, but rather becomes, a woman.
— **Simone de Beauvoir**

Birth didn't make me a mother. I became a mother slowly, over months. Some days, I'm still not a mother.

•

Winnicott's famous theory is that good enough parenting was needed for a child's development. Good enough (I can do that!) Perfection is not needed. In fact, the imperfect parent would prepare the child for the imperfect world.

Winnicott saw the mother and baby as one. There's *No such thing as a baby*. The baby can only be seen in context of the *nursing couple* (motherbaby).

311

Lisa Appignanesi says that, *One might almost conclude, to take his daring thought to its logical end, that for Winnicott there was rarely enough such a thing as a woman, since she existed entirely as part of the mother–child dyad.*

There's no such thing as a mother.

•

My friend sends me a voice message because she needs to rant. She's frustrated with her toddler. She prefixes the vent with a disclaimer. Of course, she loves her daughter, she's amazing, the best thing ever, etc. We always make sure to remind each other that we know we are lucky, that we love our children.

Why do we feel like we constantly have to prove our love, our suitability as mothers?

•

It takes a village to raise a child goes the saying.

•

The ordinary mother is good, is devoted. Devotion? To meet every need, to always be present.

Only a mother can handle the all-consuming and continuous need of the child.

The mother, to Winnicott, is a natural. Mothering is intuitive. But what of the un-ordinary mother, the mother who can't access that animal intuition?

The mother is essential. Not for what she does, but for what doing the wrong thing would cause.

If the mother failed in her ordinariness, a child could be left with a sense of unreality. An inability to form proper relationships rooted in spontaneity, instead having fantasy bonds based on perceived ideas of a role. That child would grow to live as a false self, a defensive superficial self, rather than being authentic and feeling alive.

so much depends
upon

Appignanesi notes that this feeling of unreality is caused *By a rupture or failure in early mothering or by the mother's depression.* The mother's unreality becomes the child's.

•

We're expected to be mothers the instant we lock eyes with our baby. To shed everything we were and be reborn: Madonnas.

•

Winnicott's ideas weren't aimed at belittling the role of mothering, but rather emphasising the importance of that early bond, without medical interference.

A natural mother, in sync with her child. Their bodies so recently one.

•

Every mother I know is exhausted.

That's what having kids is like! mothers tell each other.

Society tells mothers this is what it's like.

Mothers are amazing. Mothers, so loving. Mothers sacrifice everything for their children. Being a mother is a thankless job, we are told. Mothers, extraordinary creatures, phenomenal.

It's disguised as a compliment. Society appreciates the superhuman lengths mothers go to for their children. But it's no compliment, it's expectation. To be a good mother, you're expected to give every part of yourself, to spread yourself as thin as possible.

It feels like a con. A conspiracy. Society has agreed to put mothers on a pedestal, not to appreciate them, but to make sure every woman strives to reach this unrealistic expectation.

Men, generally speaking, don't feel the need to dismantle themselves when they become fathers. Their kids still know they are loved.

I want to give my son the earth. That shouldn't equal destroying myself.

•

Article 41.2.1 of the Irish constitution states, *The State recognises that by her life within the home, woman gives to the State a support without which the common good cannot be achieved.*

There have been pushes in recent years to have this repealed. It implies that a woman's place is in the home. I'm torn. It also acknowledges the domestic work.

John Bowlby, the father of attachment theory, warned of the damage caused by maternal deprivation. For Bowlby, the mother must be close (physically) and emotionally responsive for a child to form an attachment. This attachment allowed the child to grow into a healthy adult. The bond with the mother was the foundation for life. His work was built upon by Mary Ainsworth, and later William Sears, who coined the term attachment parenting.

The most important job. Ordinary. Winnicott, and later Sears, saw parenting as common sense. Yet everything depending on those first months, those first years. A mother's instincts were good enough, but must be monitored in case they weren't.

The ordinary mother, the good enough mother, came to mothering naturally. It was her instincts that were to be trusted, her body, not the mother as a woman, as a person.

so much depends
upon

•

What of the mother who can't trust her instincts? Is she less of a mother, less of an animal?

•

Mom became both less and more than human.
– **Lisa Appignanesi**

The twenty-first-century woman isn't just expected to have it all. She's expected to do it all. All by herself.

This isn't normal.

It takes a village.

We have lost our villages.

I am torn, about the constitution.

The State shall, therefore, endeavour to ensure that mothers shall not be obliged by economic necessity to engage in labour to the neglect of their duties in the home.

The mother today is expected to work both in and out of the home. We pretend domestic work doesn't exist. Without the article, would the state be obliged to provide lone parents allowance? Child maintenance payments?

Unsupported, the mother falters.

•

Van der Kolk describes a study on rhesus monkeys that examines the role of genetics in early mothering.

The uptight, anxious females don't play well with others and thus often lack social support when they give birth and are at high risk of neglecting or abusing their firstborns. But when these females belong to a stable social group, they often become diligent mothers who carefully watch out for their young.

Supported, even mothers like me will be okay.

•

A child's mother is an endless supply of love, affection, support in every way necessary. The mother's love is as certain as gravity. For the child, they don't think of it, but it holds them to the earth.

•

In *The Argonauts*, Maggie Nelson writes about *the pleasure of ordinary devotion*.

About the loss of self experienced in devotion, Nelson says:

I have never felt that way, but I'm an old mom. I had nearly four decades to become myself before experimenting with my obliteration.

I became a mother in my mid-twenties. Young enough to not be entirely comfortable in myself. Old enough to miss myself when I disappeared.

Nelson is an older mother, and an American one. There are struggles and liberties of hers that I can't understand.

I didn't just become a mother. I became an Irish mammy.

If America has MILFs, then Ireland has mammies.

The Irish mammy has become an iconic figure. Cardigans, wooden spoons, deeply loving yet stern. A caricature that we all recognise aspects of in people we know, or knew.

I post on Twitter to ask people what they think of when they hear the phrase.

Some are defensive. They hate it, as they're Irish mothers themselves. The mother as the butt of the joke.

There are light-hearted comments, images that have become jokes. Getting a cold in your kidneys, the wooden spoon, being reminded constantly to wear a coat.

One man, a poet older than my parents but younger than

their parents, messages me to express his dislike of the term. It makes him think of *enslaved women* and a generation of men who were *clueless* on the domestic front. I think of some men I've known who couldn't load dishwashers, didn't do laundry, never learned to cook. So used to adoration that no amount of love would be enough for them. I think of their mothers, praising them, putting them on a pedestal.

If a mother must dismantle herself to be a mother, what happens when their children grow up? When your whole life is your child, who can judge you for being overbearing?

The Irish mammy comes from many of our own mothers, grandmothers, great-grandmothers. At a time, in a culture, when men were put first. Women were to put them first. Fathers and sons were served first at the dinner table.

A doula from our town sees the term affectionately:

Baking soda bread, homemade jam and apple tart. Washing on the line on a breezy day, spit on a thumb to clean your face as a child, reminding you money doesn't grow on trees and what happened in her day. I love my Irish Mammy.

A writer, a woman, older than my mother, younger than my grandmother, replies with, *Diverse conversations, open mindedness, being her own woman.*

Another, my age, *Sensible working-class women.* I hadn't thought of the class aspect before.

I think of the matriarchs in my family. My father's grandmother who raised all of her children after her husband died. A working-class family, my grandfather was born in a tenement. His mother moved the family to England, to give them a better chance.

My mother's mother. Orphaned in her teens. She married

my grandfather in her twenties. Raised six daughters in a county where neither of them had family. My grandfather worked. At one stage she had a three-year-old, a two-year-old, a one-year-old, and a newborn. At home alone all day.

I think of the poet's phrase again, *enslaved women*.

•

The flawed mother, the mother who could not provide a stable beginning, the appropriate emotional responses, could be problematic just by being absent.

William Sears is opposed to the mother returning to work:

Mothers choose to go back to their jobs quickly simply because they don't understand how disruptive that is to the well-being of their babies. So many babies in our culture are not being cared for in the way God designed, and we as a nation are paying the price.

As if the baby will not leave the womb. Motherbaby.

•

The pedestal of the maternal ideal. Suffocated with praise. I can dress it up, aim for the unachievable. Fail.

•

I ask the baby's father.

Quick, word association, Irish Mammy.

Strong, he says.

·

The first B of the seven Bs of attachment parenting. Birth bonding. The idea that there's a brief window after birth when the baby is most susceptible to bonding. That the baby imprints like a goose. Sears advises against analgesics for the mother, so as not to interrupt the birth bonding.

so much depends
upon

·

The bond, between mother and child, is instinctual, instant. After birth, there will be relief, euphoria, a new face close to mine that I have, instinctually, always known.

As we enter this world, we scream to announce our presence. Someone immediately engages with us, bathes us, swaddles us, and fills our stomachs, and, best of all, our mother may put us on her belly or breast for delicious skin-to-skin contact.

The beginning of a secure bond. More instant and mystical than any romantic love.

The importance of it is reiterated, *skin to skin for as long as possible!*

But

Sedated, we are cheated out of this perfect beginning. I did not want to add to my baby's disadvantages.

·

I don't know what went wrong in me. What sways me off balance. When it happened. Nothing happened. Genetic? Maybe.

Will being my child be another of his disadvantages? What lives in my blood, that could carry down to him?

It's now thought that genes aren't set in stone. We may carry the fibres of fate in our blood, but our worlds weave them as we grow.

Safe and protective early relationships are critical to protect children from long-term problems. In addition, even parents with their own genetic vulnerabilities can pass on that protection to the next generation provided that they are given the right support.

It's not all down to genetics.

Lack of safety within the early caregiving relationship led to an impaired sense of inner reality, excessive clinging, and self-damaging behavior: Poverty, single parenthood, or maternal psychiatric symptoms did not predict these symptoms.

It's not who I am, it's what I do.

Is this better or worse? Either way, it's on me now.

The therapist tells me a child only needs one stable parent. One person. It's the attachment that matters.

Yet, when you don't feel present, when you feel out of time entirely, how are you supposed to be the perfect mother?

Winnicott's imperfect perfect mother, as long as she can be mentally, emotionally present, that's enough. (And if it's the only thing you can't do?)

When infants and young children notice that their mothers are not fully engaged with them, they become nervous.

How many new mothers are left traumatised from birth and its aftermath, unable to feel present in their new world?

(Alone on the ward. Aching and terrified. Knowing it was twelve hours until I would have the support of family. A small precious life fluttering beside me.)

Do current societal structures leave us open to it?

While all parents need all the help they can get to help raise secure children, traumatized parents, in particular, need help to be attuned to their children's needs.

•

We have the choice, now, to become mothers. Only as recently as the year before my son was born, women in Ireland were forced to continue pregnancies they didn't want.

I see aspects of Irish mammydom that I want to be. I want to cook for my child. I want him to roll his eyes at my worrying, but know that he has to do what I say anyway. I want him to know I'd do anything in the world to keep him safe and happy.

I don't want to grow old over a stove. I don't want to be the butt of jokes I'm not in on. I don't want to lose myself.

•

A child should be able to take their parents' love and devotion for granted. A child should never question that they are loved. That doesn't mean a child should learn that their mother's time has no value. That their lives revolve around their children's needs. A mother isn't to be ignored, demanded from, used. A mother is not a resource to be drained.

It takes a village.

It's not a child's responsibility to replenish a mother's energy. She needs a support system. A village.

•

so much depends
upon

•

It takes a village. Have (do) it all.

•

Mamó says, *They were doing it all, but they were doing it in small town Ireland, in co. with a lot more people.*

The woman has lost her village. Now, a mother's mother is her village.

•

The mother who does everything is primed to do everything wrong.

Yet, being a human is to be flawed. Can any and all of our flaws be blamed on our mothers? Unless we aim to raise a flawless person (the divine mother, her incorruptible son), there will always be something to blame on mothers.

My mother's love has given me confidence I probably didn't deserve. Even in the worst times in my life, I have had a foundation of security in myself from the love and support she has given me.

I take my mother for granted. I think I always have.

I do it.

Mum, can you?

Mum, would you hold the baby while I?

If I'm not careful, the cycle will continue.

(So! Much! Depends!

Upon!)

•

My mother, letting me be a child again, so that I can become a mother.

•

I am devoted to my son. It is extraordinary. I hope he will grow up secure in the wonder of this love, knowing the mothers in his life are whole, full people, just like him.

+9

The baby is nine months old.

When the baby turns nine months old, I know I have to stop writing about him. At least for now, in this way.

He has lived in the world as long as he lived in my body.

When he cries now, which is rarely, I am not afraid. It is out of frustration, exhaustion, or a dozen other nuanced variations of emotions that he has.

He makes decisions, has clear preferences. Soon there will be words amongst the gabbling chat of his baby phonemes.

This is to say, he is not mine now. Our relationship has become just that, a relationship between two people. One more loving and dependent than any other, but a distinct connection between two separate entities.

He is, as I suspected, a whole wonderful person.

When it's just the two of us, I don't feel alone anymore. (I'm not. I haven't been alone for eighteen months, more. Yet there are parts of that never aloneness that only reveal a vulnerability I'd rather hide.) I have company, this small friend who I get to introduce to the world.

Somewhere between the nine- and ten-month mark, the mirror image of his conception, I know I have to stop writing about him. At least in this way, my reflection in him.

•

The baby's favourite thing to do is sit on my lap and interact with other people. This is what mothers are for, I think. Comfort, security, a place to get to know the world from.

I kiss the back of his head as he makes faces at his grandmother. His personality becomes more pronounced every day. I've started to write poetry again. Just little bits of it. The country has been in lockdown for over a month. I sleep a little more. I have to stop writing about the baby now. Even typing one handed while his cheek turns pink against my chest. He's been in my arms as long as he was in my body. The further he grows from me, the more of a betrayal the writing feels. He's not mine. Not in that way.

Thirty-Nine Weeks and Two Days. Due to these particular months, exactly nine months since he was born.

He is of the world now. As much time in air as water.

•

People forget that postnatal depression does not cause itself. It's an effect.

The storm of circumstance.

Mad? How could I not be.

•

In the depths of it, sobbing.

My wisest friend says:

You are living your choices.

I haven't just run away.

Leaving behind sensible choices. The offices, the apartment, the men. The almost rights. I've run away from them, confident in the direction of my desires.

Geared on by the senseless self-belief my parents instilled in me.

I've run towards the things I want.

Poetry

Home

Motherhood

My modest glorious wants.

•

Maybe this, then, is why I write. To remember the days, the moments. Not just how they look, from the outside, but how I felt.

My son, I love my days with you so much I want to capture them. They are so precious, I'm afraid of doing it wrong. I want to freeze it all, but continue along, simultaneously. I want to meet you as an adult, hear the wonderful things you think, but hold you in my arms for ever.

Soon we will go home. The new home. Although I don't know it yet, in the months to come, we will leave there too. In my running, I will return. A returning, a new way (for me) of growing.

If I am to be a foundation, I must learn stillness.

Now, I can build on the joy of my own beginnings.

My mother pretends to sneeze to make the baby laugh. He laughs again and again. They are caught in it, the breathless hilarious joy of the moment.

I love that she loves him as much as I do. I love that he will love her as much as I do. I love that, without me, their bond thrives anyway.

•

You wait for the watershed, the reset, the chance to make the mistakes right. Diagnosis or treatment or quitting drinking or moving or meeting a guy or having a child. The climax. The point everything changes.

Even the realisation isn't delivered divinely, just slowly acknowledged. Change is glacial.

Life seems to be a series of small epiphanies.

I walk the grounds of my parents' garden. This place has pulled me back time and time again. This province. This county. This garden. I exhale fully here, with the raindrops clinging to the ash leaves, a mistiness to the air.

To leave only to come home again (nothing here is new).

The smell of grass and sweet sleep is all around. The neighbour's farmland encroaches. I am not a farm girl, but I grew up watching the cows in the field. I named them, patted their wet noses. I couldn't understand that anyone could raise them from babies and sell them for meat. It was the first way humanity baffled me.

In late spring the calves are released into the fields with their mothers. The cows come first; the calves have been held back for tagging or dehorning, or one of the many other logistical intrusions that affects the young of agriculturally bred animals. The cows huddle in a corner of the field. Calves cluster towards them, like flies to the proverbial. Slowly they spread out, filling the bright green of the field.

After putting the baby to bed I walk the field. The air has turned chilly. The daisies have closed and the stone walls are a soft gold with the dropping sun. There's just the one cow and her calf left within view; the rest have dispersed across the acres.

The cow's udders are swollen. One significantly more than the others. It hangs low enough to brush the tops of the dandelions. The calf trips alongside her, suckling when he can. The cow, irritated (I'm projecting), walks regardless of the calf's attachment.

Stretchy skin. Veins.

Apparently, people get angry at vegans for comparing women to cows. They think it's insulting.

I've seen it on Twitter. The blind fury.

There aren't a lot of things people don't get angry about on Twitter.

It's a misunderstood comparison. There's much more to it than milk.

+3

We're walking along the river. I don't think I'm pushing the buggy. Maybe he is. Maybe the baby is at home, being minded by my visiting parents.

I say to him:

You know, I'm not in pain.

What?

Right now. I'm not in any pain.

I stop, tense, relax. Close my eyes. Just in case I'm missing something.

Nope. No pain. For the first time in what, ten weeks?

More like halfway through pregnancy, when the leg thing started.

Oh, yeah.

Mad.

Mad.

Milk (-120, 0, +3)

He should have done this months ago, the vet told me in the cab of the van as he prepared his equipment. Gloves, a can of disinfectant, a saw with orange specs across the blade.

I was sixteen, doing work experience with the local vet. I had hoped for hand-feeding kittens, and vaccinating puppies, but the animals in the afternoon clinic were usually old, broken, sick. The failing body is the medic's bread and butter.

In the mornings, we rode around the county making calls to farms. Half remembered details. Bessie, a lone cow on a bed of straw, her farmer shhhing to calm her. The cow in the crush with the breach calf, where a choice between saving the mother or young had to be made. Trying to shoot a stained medicine into the corner of a heifer's mouth with a giant plastic syringe.

Gates, clamps, waving arms. Tricks and hisses and force. You can't reason with an animal.

The clearest day. A small concrete yard up a hill, spruce trees guarding the house from the relentless westerly wind. The slatted house opened onto the yard, about thirty cattle looking out. Yearlings, ready to go to the mart, except for their horns. Off-white, curling to a sharp point. It made something wild of them, the cows, previously as common and innocuous to me as trees, as houses, as clouds dotting the sky.

He should have done this months ago.

I asked, *It doesn't hurt them, does it?*

The vet, a kind but pragmatic man, suggested I stay out of the barn for this visit.

The concrete was slick with brown and green of mud and shit trodden down by hooves and wellingtons. The yard had small drains set into the concrete. Brownish water trickled down them.

The sharp screech of metal on bone. The guttural scream of an animal in more pain than it can handle.

•

My mother raised me vegetarian. Eating meat, flesh, is incomprehensible to me. When I was a child, I'd explain it (to parents of friends who were frustrated by my not eating the burgers, waitresses who insisted fish was for vegetarians, teachers who told me carnivores existed in nature) as, *I don't want to cause pain when I understand what it is to feel pain.*

•

There is a violence in surgical birth I didn't expect. New to me. Too many hands on my body. Inescapable pain.

•

It is illegal in Ireland to dehorn an animal without local anaesthetic. The strength, or effectiveness, of the anaesthetic does not seem to be specified.

Perhaps it's the separation, or the rawness of this new relationship. New exposure to violence. Where there was movement, soft flows and heartbeat, now a wound, a sharp ache.

Images flash in front of me like premonitions. A raving man in the neonatal unit, slicing newborn bellies in two. Tripping over my own feet, soft skull on tiles, blood flowing.

I could not control my body. My mind follows.

•

I thought he would be a girl. I'd never imagined having a son.

This small boy. Tiny man.

•

The male calves of dairy cows can't be bred for beef or dairy. Their lack of financial value means they are either killed not long after birth, or exported for veal. Many agree that killing at birth is the kinder of the two fates.

•

My son's first cry, slicing white pain.

•

The noise kept coming.

The concrete channels of the farmyard flowed with blood. Bright crimson lapping its way over the muck, like a quick flow of lava over earth. I thought of Paris, the guillotine. There is more blood than seems reasonable for an animal to lose and remain alive.

•

Can you feel that? You can't feel that.

Calves of dairy cows are taken from their mothers within twenty-four hours of their birth. They are fed milk substitutes. The milk their mothers make for them with their bodies goes to us.

•

In the cot at night the baby bucks and cries. His stomach is causing him discomfort. Hurting him. We bring him to hospital. He's three months old. Babies under six months get redirected to A&E. For efficiency, they keep us in overnight.

Him, but us really. I go where he goes. We sleep in a room with cartoons on the wall.

I swallow balls of panic. I don't have the motion detector that beeps to tell me he is breathing. This is the place where things are bad. I wait for it to get bright.

We are discharged in the morning.

I read about cow's milk protein allergies online. It's not uncommon in babies his age, and the symptoms line up. In every thread I read, someone brings up that milk made for baby cattle isn't intended for humans. Images of calves. The unnatural doesn't alarm me, unless it's a source of pain.

I suggest to the doctor that this may be the source of his obvious physical discomfort. The doctor rolls his eyes and warns of mothers and their internet addiction.

(*A mother knows best!*)

After two months of inconclusive testing, he diagnoses a milk protein allergy. The protein passes from any dairy I consume into my milk. His sole food source, what I make for him with my body, is causing him pain. I take this next step towards veganism. I cut out milk, cheese, yoghurt. I check ingredients on jars, learn to make cheese out of cashews. I don't know if I notice a reduction in symptoms without dairy in my diet. It's hard to remember each stage as the next arrives.

Experts say that the cessation of commercial animal farming will be necessary to decrease the effects of climate change and maintain human civilisation on earth.

I start to follow sustainability hashtags on Instagram. Most of my recipes involve oats. When I can't sleep, I look on property websites for rural holdings with land. I imagine polytunnels full of carrots, aubergine, courgettes, tomatoes, peas, runner beans, avocados. Hens run in and out of the kitchen and I bake using rapeseed oil and oat milk.

The hope of personal responsibility.

If I can eradicate dairy from our diet, maybe I can stop the damage the industry is doing from reaching our home.

If I can learn how to grow vegetables, maybe the climate crisis will bypass Ireland.

If I can control *this one thing*, maybe I can keep us safe.

In the field next to my parents' house there's a cattle crush, an enclosure that keeps the animal restrained while being examined by a vet or other professional. The owner of this field, a farmer, often kept cows in the crush overnight before a vet was coming. This was beside the field in which calves were kept before being taken away.

•

What makes us animal: movement, sex, blood? (Mammal: Milk.)

What makes us human: language, consciousness, technology?

•

The vet started his days before 8 a.m. with a trip to the abattoir to test the cattle for diseases that were dangerous to humans if consumed through the meat.

I found it strange that the man who tickled our dog's ears when giving her vaccines could feel the breath and shiver of a cow under his hands, knowing it was headed for slaughter within the hour.

•

The baby's new face pushed to mine.

The man with his hands in the cavity of my abdomen says: *The patient cannot tolerate the sensation.*

•

The body likes to remind me that I'm an animal. The delicate systems that keep me moving, so easily thrown off. Memory, barely there. Pain, robbing me of my convictions. Milk, sweat, blood, tears. Need for water.

I worry love is just an instinct.

•

Those first hours.

A latch on my breast, the baby being taken to the nurse's station. Most of the memories didn't form, my head woozy from anaesthetic.

The days after.

The baby is small and needs feeding. My milk won't come. They give him formula. Little branded plastic bottles. He won't latch to me. The midwives tell me it's confidence.

•

The maternity ward is filled with babies' cries. They become background noise, the same as the beeping of blood pressure monitors, the clack of midwives' steps. None of these cries are my baby.

Does having a baby make you sympathetic to all those cries? my mother asks.

No, I say, *they don't make me feel anything.*

•

Mamó tells me:

I was told by the doctor before, 'No reason not to have an epidural.'

Went in and, 'Oh you don't want that missus.'

I had no time to feel labour pains that time, I was too busy fighting with the doctor.

•

They bring the baby to me. Visiting hours are over, it's just the two of us for the night. *Feed every three hours*, I am told. *Remember, confidence!*

I tuck the baby to my body. He seems to drink, to sleep. I try to sleep too, know that I won't. He wakes. Memory serves to silence the scene. I ring the bell for help. I wish it weren't the middle of the night. That we weren't alone.

He's fine.

I think he's shaking, though? Do you see that.

No, if you're feeding him, I'm sure he's fine.

I am, I'm trying, but, I'm not sure he's getting the milk?

They take the baby back.

•

I hook myself up to the hospital machines and watch as the milk spurts into the small plastic bottles. I label them with the baby's name and bring them to him, still warm. It's a long walk down two hallways from the maternity ward to NICU. Longer still with a barely closed abdominal wound. I make the journey every three hours.

Every step shifts the sewn together muscles. I catch the pain between my teeth.

·

In 2019, Alexander Green, a researcher at Sydney University, published her findings that cows respond to positive and negative emotional prompts with individual voice. *'It is like she is building a Google translate for cows,'* said Associate Professor Cameron Clark, Ms Green's academic supervisor. Cows have their own voice. Language, so preciously human, so universal. They express feelings based on experience. *Cattle mother–offspring contact calls encode individual-identity information.* The cow knows her calf's cry.

·

The late summer nights of my youth were peppered with the desperate lowing of separated mothers and children.

·

After two days, the baby is wheeled to my bedside in his plastic cradle. He seems smaller every time I see him. I don't feel like I'll be allowed to keep him.

Having grown used to the ease of silicone teats, he will not latch. Every three hours I limp to the nursing room, pump each breast until the bottle is full, and shuffle back to the ward. My mother stays with the baby. They push the limits of visiting hours to keep my panic at bay.

At night I must leave him in the room alone. He sleeps.

From the nursing chair I can hear only the shhhing hiss of milk on plastic. Bottle full, I step into the hallway to his scream. Unmistakably his. Unbearable to only me. I run for the first time in months. I can feel the blade's work redoing itself, a slash with each step.

The high pitch of my son's early cries, a helpless animal. Me, the one thing in his world that could bring comfort, unable to.

I lift him, frantic, from the cot. He is too young for tears. Only a look of great confusion and pain. He wants the security of his mother's body. Bottle to his lips, he stills again.

My mother talks about the night the baby was born. The hours after.

You were serene, she says, *I was so impressed. It took me ages to realise it's cause you were out of your bin on all the morphine.*

+5

I haven't seen the video before. But I filmed it. The date of the file is the day after his date of birth. The time, early morning, though many would see it as late at night. It's a close up of his face, gentle sucking at my breast, the room the colour of the blueish grey of a summer predawn. He's a few hours old, it's just the two of us.

Later

Home, new home, again.

•

I walk our morning route. The new already feeling old. The baby sits up in the buggy. When we're outside, around the unfamiliar, his eyes are rounder, his mouth disappears entirely. He's unselfconscious, taking everything in.

Walking the baby I tell him about trees, ivy, the shells of fledglings, the history of the Catholic Church in Ireland. He doesn't understand, but I am practising. Practising the sort of parent I want to be.

The new home on the brink of being old. A home we will not stay in, we will make a home anew, somewhere old, walking and rewalking the same r(outes)(oots). Together.

I can think of these things now. I don't feel trapped in my body. My body that has done so much, for me, for us. I must look after it, for me, for us.

Looking up at the trees, the leaves the same now as when he was born. Like nothing has changed. As if the curl and rot and quiet of it all was not unique, as if every new leaf doesn't unfold with relief at its first gulp of sunlight.

Acknowledgements

The number of thanks due could double the length of this book. I will try to keep it brief. This book would not exist in its current form without any of the following people.

Thank you to my agent, Marianne Gunn O'Connor, whose talent is rivalled only by her kindness.

My editor, Gillian Fitzgerald-Kelly, Laura Carr, Siobhan Slattery, and everyone at Picador for giving this book such care and the best home I could have imagined.

JP McManus, Roger Downer, Diana McCabe, and everyone at All Ireland Scholarships. Where I'd be without your generosity, I don't know.

Sinéad Gleeson, Joseph O'Connor, and Donal Ryan for choosing an early extract of this book as the winning entry of the AIS creative writing competition, and for being so generous with your kind words. That extract, 'Window', was subsequently published in RTÉ culture. A second extract, 'Milk', was published in *Banshee* issue #12.

Many of the first fragments that became *Milk* emerged from discussions at the Benchmark project with the Linenhall Arts Centre. Thank you to all at the Linenhall then and now, especially Orla Henihan and Bernadette Greenan, and to Mike McCormack and the Crows Foot writers.

The Arts Council of Ireland for a literature bursary that

allowed me the time to complete the first draft of this manuscript.

Thanks are due to the many healthcare professionals, friendly faces, and assorted people mentioned in this book, whose kindness and generosity made the experience of pregnancy and new motherhood a little easier.

I have been exceptionally fortunate to have had many mentors, friends, and those who were both, who have supported me to this point. I am exceptionally grateful to you all. I would like to pay special thanks to Morag Prunty and Sarah Moore Fitzgerald.

To Jenny, for getting it, and to Ingrid and Seanín, for the heads-up.

Thank you to Rúairí, without whose hospitable ear and discerning eye this book might never have gotten off the ground. To Daniel, for the ongoing camaraderie, plotting, and love.

Thank you to my family, especially my Mamó for her invaluable contributions to this book.

To my parents, Éadaoin and Paul, endless thanks, none of this would be possible without you.

E, when you are old enough to read this book, thank you for the life you've given me. I love you.

Notes

10 **My body, my life, became the landscape of my son's life** . . . Manguso, *Two Kinds of Decay*.

12 **MOTHER is our point of origin** . . . Zambreno, *Book of Mutter*.

26 **Pumping milk is, for many women, a sharply private activity** . . . Nelson, *The Argonauts*.

28 **Breastfeeding and class were connected** . . . Stevens et al., 'A History of Infant Feeding'.

29 **Breastfeeding rates strongly correlate to maternal education** . . . 'Breastfeeding in a Healthy Ireland', Health Service Breastfeeding Action Plan 2016–2021: https://www.hse.ie/eng/about/who/healthwellbeing/healthy-ireland/publications/breastfeeding-in-a-healthy-ireland.pdf [accessed 14 July 2022].

30 **By 2016, Irish breastfeeding initiation rates were 56.9 per cent** . . . Perinatal Statistics Report 2016, Healthcare Pricing Office, Health Service Executive, October 2018.

38 **Not to take pictures of one's children** . . . Sontag, *On Photography*.

47 **The main reason women gave for choosing NOT to breastfeed** . . . https://www.inmo.ie/Magazine Article/PrintArticle/7780 [accessed 10 August 2022].

47   **Negative perceptions of breastfeeding including**
      . . . 'Breastfeeding in a Healthy Ireland', Health Service
      Breastfeeding Action Plan 2016–2021: https://www.
      hse.ie/eng/about/who/healthwellbeing/healthy-ireland/
      publications/breastfeeding-in-a-healthy-ireland.pdf
      [accessed 14 July 2022].

51   **I read somewhere that it is inappropriate . . .**
      Cusk, *A Life's Work*.

52   **The principles of the IMBCIO are . . .** http://imb
      co.weebly.com/the-initiative.html [accessed 9 August
      2022].

57   **In 2017, an image listing REASONS FOR**
      ADMISSION went viral . . . https://dangerous
      minds.net/comments/list_of_reasons_for_admission_
      to_an_insane_asylum [accessed 9 August 2022].

68   **I felt as you do after trauma . . .** Allardice, Lisa,
      'Tiger King and a bloody mary: Hilary Mantel,
      Simon Armitage and other writers on lockdown
      life', *The Guardian* (3 April 2020): https://www.
      theguardian.com/books/2020/apr/03/corona-crisis
      -tiger-king-lockdown-life-hilary-mantel-simon-
      armitage-julian-barnes-anne-enright-jeannette-
      winterson-diane-evans

68   **The format of a narrative presented in fragments**
      . . . Molk, 'Maternal Landscapes', in May, *The Best,*
      Most Awful Job.

87   **Livestock emissions make up 14.5 per cent . . .**
      Food and Agricultural Organisation of the United
      Nations: www.fao.org/news/story/en/item/197623/
      icode/ [accessed 9 August 2022].

87 **Climate scientists agree that society transitioning**
. . . Clark et al., 'Global food system emissions', *Science*.

87 **In 1978, the European Commission introduced**
. . . The National Dairy Council: https://ndc.ie/
about-us/our-history/ [accessed 9 August 2022].

90 **And then, since they** . . . Frost, 'Out, Out', *Collected
Poems of Robert Frost* (Henry Holt & Company, 1942):
https://www.poetryfoundation.org/poems/53087/
out-out [accessed 9 August 2022].

91 **A photograph is always invisible** . . . Barthes,
Camera Lucida.

100 **The Operator is the Photographer** . . . Ibid.

101 **And the person or thing photographed is the
target** . . . Ibid.

101 **Now, once I feel myself observed** . . . Ibid.

102 **No doubt it is metaphorically that I derive** . . .
Ibid.

103 **Each time I am (or let myself be) photographed**
. . . Ibid.

103 **In every photograph:** . . . Ibid.

118 **A witch would come in the night** . . . Approximately
740,000 pages (288,000 pages in the pupils' original
exercise books; 451,000 pages in bound volumes) of
folklore and local tradition were compiled by pupils
from 5,000 primary schools in the Irish Free State
between 1937 and 1939. This collecting scheme was
initiated by the Irish Folklore Commission, under the
direction of Séamus Ó Duilearga and Séan Ó
Súilleabháin, Honorary Director and Registrar of the
Commission respectively, and was heavily dependent

on the cooperation of the Department of Education and the Irish National Teachers' Organization. It was originally to run from 1937 to 1938 but was extended to 1939 in specific cases. For the duration of the project, more than 50,000 schoolchildren from 5,000 schools in the 26 counties of the Irish Free State were enlisted to collect folklore in their home districts. This included oral history, topographical information, folktales and legends, riddles and proverbs, games and pastimes, trades and crafts. The children recorded this material from their parents, grandparents and neighbours. The scheme resulted in the creation of over half a million manuscript pages and is generally referred to as '*Bailiúchán na Scol*' or 'The Schools' Collection'. There are 1,128 volumes, numbered and bound, in the Collection. A title page prefaces material from each school, giving the name of the school, the parish, the barony, the county and the teacher. A further collection of approximately 40,000 of the children's original copybooks are stored at the NFC: https://www.duchas.ie/en/cbes/4713253/4711791/4743668 [accessed 9 August 2022].

118 **Long ago it was the custom . . .** Ibid.

118 **The first three days of May . . .** Ibid.

119 **Long ago the Milesians . . .** Ibid.

119 **Every May Day since this . . .** Ibid.

148 **A 2001 study called 'The Girl Who Cried Pain'** . . . Jamison, *The Empathy Exams*.

148 **Evidence suggests that healthcare staff routinely** . . . Williams, Amanda C. de C., 'Gender pain gap: Why

stereotypes are still harming women's health', *The Independent* (13 April 2021): www.independent.co.uk/health_and_wellbeing/women-pain-underestimated-male-stereotypes-b1828978.html

148 **Gender stereotypes are particularly decisive in the . . .** Ibid.

149 **Failures in maternity care are not just about . . .** Sodha, Sonia, 'No evidence and little research – it's no wonder that women and babies continue to die', *The Observer* (4 July 2021): www.theguardian.com/commentisfree/2021/jul/04/as-long-as-sexism-lies-at-the-heart-of-childcare-babies-and-women-will-continue-to-die.

168 **Hysteria, the first female disease . . .** Tasca, Cecilia, Rapetti, Mariangela, et al., 'Women and Hysteria in the History of Mental Health', *Clinical Practice and Epidemiology in Mental Health* (2012): www.ncbi.nlm.nih.gov/pmc/articles/PMC3480686/

169 **Hysteria is no longer considered a valid diagnosis . . .** Ibid.

186 **When extremely sleep deprived . . .** Zambreno, *Book of Mutter.*

196 **Feeling of cosmic panic . . .** Zapffe, Peter Wessel, 'The Last Messiah', tr. Gisle R. Tangenes, *Janus* No.9 (1933).

196 **Most people learn to save themselves . . .** Ibid.

222 **To be a housewife, in the old mold, . . .** Zambreno, *Book of Mutter.*

231 **I wrote so I could say I was truly paying attention . . .** Manguso, *Ongoingness.*

232 **Living in a dream of the future is considered**
. . . Ibid.

237 **The lesser, superficial self, rooted in our perception . . .** Winnicott, *The Maturational Processes and the
Facilitating Environment.*

238 **I've been thinking with my guts since I was
fourteen years old . . .** Hornby, *High Fidelity.*

238 **The woman has lost her village . . .** 'The Science
of Families', *Time* magazine (September 2018): https://
books.google.ie/books?id=vaxwDwAAQBAJ&lpg
=PT9&ots=MciUYDvEur&dq=stay%20at%20home%

242 **Trauma, by definition, is unbearable . . .** van der
Kolk, *The Body Keeps the Score.*

242 **The brain keeps secreting stress chemicals . . .**
Ibid.

242 **The effects of trauma are not necessarily
different from— . . .** Ibid.

242 **Trauma is not just an event that took place . . .**
Ibid.

243 **We become like conditioned animals: . . .** Ibid.

243 **In response to the trauma itself, and in coping
with the dread . . .** Ibid.

245 **10 things to know about perinatal health . . .**
https://www.hse.ie/eng/services/news/media/pressrel/
10-things-to-know-about-perinatal-mental-health.html
[accessed 9 August 2022].

248 **I have been your slave! . . .** Zambreno, *Book of
Mutter.*

249 **There is a certain consistency of complaint . . .**
Galchen, *Little Labours.*

250 **All my childhood I remember my mother cleaning** . . . Zambreno, *Book of Mutter*.

257 **Needing to have reality confirmed and experience enhanced** . . . Sontag, *On Photography*.

279 **A gloomy abode of mingled want,** . . . Carr, *The Stranger in Ireland*.

290 **There's a prevalent fear that engaging artistically** . . . Molk, 'Maternal Landscapes', in May, *The Best, Most Awful Job*.

290 **All human life on the planet is born of woman** . . . Rich, *Of Woman Born*.

291 **Novels and memoirs by women writing artfully and with vulnerability** . . . Molk, 'Maternal Landscapes' in May, *The Best, Most Awful Job*.

292 **These books became the close friends** . . . Ibid.

295 **They weren't texts so much as talismans** . . . Sudjic, *Exposure*.

302 **Although I found her work interesting** . . . Chesler, *With Child*.

305 **Child: I'll search for Mothers, dead and alive, to guide me** . . . **'And who could be closer than we two?'** . . . Ibid.

309 **so much depends / upon / a red wheel** . . . Williams, 'The Red Wheelbarrow', in *The Collected Poems of William Carlos Williams, Volume I: 1909– 1939*.

310 **Winnicott made babies interesting** . . . Appignanesi, *Mad, Bad, and Sad*.

310 **Undoubtedly a world war, followed within a single** . . . Ibid.

310 **In the culture at large into which Klein's complex hypotheses** . . . Ibid.

310 **Ordinary good mother** . . . **devoted to her infant.** Winnicott, *The Child, the Family, and the Outside World.*

311 **One is not born, but rather becomes, a woman.** de Beauvoir, *The Second Sex.*

311 **No such thing as a baby.** Winnicott, *The Child, the Family, and the Outside World.*

312 **One might almost conclude, to take his daring thought to** . . . Appignanesi, *Mad, Bad, and Sad.*

313 **By a rupture or failure in early mothering** . . . Ibid.

315 **Mom became both less and more than human.** Ibid.

316 **The uptight, anxious females don't play well with others** . . . van der Kolk, *The Body Keeps the Score.*

317 **I have never felt that way, but I'm an old mom** . . . Nelson, *The Argonauts.*

319 **Mothers choose to go back to their jobs quickly** . . . Sears, *The Complete Book of Christian Parenting and Child Care.*

320 **As we enter this world, we scream to announce our presence** . . . van der Kolk, *The Body Keeps the Score.*

321 **Safe and protective early relationships** . . . Ibid.

321 **Lack of safety within the early caregiving relationship** . . . Ibid.

321 **When infants and young children notice that their mothers** . . . Ibid.

322 **While all parents need all the help** . . . Ibid.

354

333 **It is illegal in Ireland to dehorn an animal . . .** Earley, B., McGee, M., et al., 'Calf disbudding and castration', *Veterinary Ireland Journal* (2019), 9(5): 269–71.

334 **Many agree that killing at birth is the kinder . . .** Kevany, Sophie & Busby, Mattha, '"It would be kinder to shoot them": Ireland's calves set for live export', *The Guardian* (20 January 2020): www.theguardian.com/environment/2020/jan/20/it-would-be-kinder-to-shoot-them-irelands-calves-set-for-live-export

340 **'It is like she is building a Google translate for cows,' . . .** Green, Alexandra, Clark, Cameron, Livio, Favaro, et al., 'Vocal individuality of Holstein-Friesian cattle is maintained across putatively positive and negative farming contexts', *Scientific Reports* (2019), 9(18468): https://www.nature.com/articles/s41598-019-54968-4 [accessed 9 August 2022].

340 **Cattle mother–offspring contact calls encode . . .** Ibid.

Bibliography

Appignanesi, Lisa, *Mad, Bad, and Sad: A History of Women and the Mind Doctors from 1800 to the Present* (Little, Brown Book Group, 2009)

Barthes, Roland, *Camera Lucida*, tr. Richard Howard (Vintage, 1993)

Baudrillard, Jean, *Simulacra and Simulation* (University of Michigan Press, 1994)

de Beauvoir, Simone, *The Second Sex* (Vintage, 2015)

Carr, John, *The Stranger in Ireland, Or, a Tour in the Southern and Western Parts of That Country in the Year 1805* (Andesite Press, 2015)

Chesler, Phyllis, *With Child: A Diary of Motherhood* (Chicago Review Press, 2018)

Clark, Michael, A., et al., 'Global food system emissions could preclude achieving the $1.5°$ and $2°$ climate change targets', *Science* (2020), 370(6517): 705–8.

Cusk, Rachel, *A Life's Work* (Faber & Faber, 2001)

Galchen, Rivka, *Little Labours* (Fourth Estate, 2017)

Gilman, Charlotte Perkins, *The Yellow Wallpaper, Herland, and Selected Writings* (Penguin Classics, 2010)

Hornby, Nick, *High Fidelity* (Penguin, 1995)

Jamison, Leslie, *The Empathy Exams* (Granta Books, 2015)

Kilroy, Claire, 'F for Phone', *Winter Pages*, Volume 1 (Curlew Editions, 2015)

Manguso, Sarah, *Ongoingness: The end of a diary* (Picador, 2018)

————, *Two Kinds of Decay* (Granta Books, 2011)

May, Katherine (ed.), *The Best, Most Awful Job: Twenty Writers Talk Honestly About Motherhood* (Elliot & Thompson, 2020)

Molk, Carolina Alvarado, 'Maternal Landscapes', in May, Katherine (ed.) *The Best, Most Awful Job: Twenty Writers Talk Honestly About Motherhood* (Elliot & Thompson, 2020)

Nelson, Maggie, *The Argonauts* (Graywolf Press, 2016)

Porter, Max, *Grief Is the Thing with Feathers* (Faber & Faber, 2015)

Rich, Adrienne, *Of Woman Born: Motherhood as Experience and Institution* (W. W. Norton & Company, 2021)

Riley, Denise, *Time Lived, Without Its Flow* (Picador, 2019)

Sears, William, *The Complete Book of Christian Parenting and Child Care* (B&H Books, 1997)

Sontag, Susan, *On Photography* (Farrar, Straus and Giroux, 1977)

Stevens, Emily, Patrick, Thelma, et al., 'A History of Infant Feeding', *The Journal of Perinatal Education* (2009), 18(2): 32–9.

Sudjic, Olivia, *Exposure* (Peninsula Press, 2018)

van der Kolk, Bessel, *The Body Keeps the Score: Mind, Brain and the Body in the Transformation of Trauma* (Penguin, 2015)

Williams, William Carlos, 'The Red Wheelbarrow', in *The Collected Poems of William Carlos Williams, Volume I: 1909–1939* (New Directions Publishing Corporation, 1938)

Winnicott, D. W., 'Ego Distortion in Terms of True and False Self', in *The Maturational Processes and the Facilitating Environment: Studies in the Theory of Emotional Development* (Routledge, 1984)

———, *The Child, the Family, and the Outside World* (Penguin Classics, 2021)

Zambreno, Kate, *Book of Mutter* (Semiotexte, 2017)

Permissions Acknowledgements

The publisher gratefully acknowledges the following for permission to reproduce extracts from these works:

With grateful acknowledgement for permission to reprint from *Two Kinds of Decay* by Sarah Manguso (Granta Books, 2011); *Ongoingness: The end of a diary* by Sarah Manguso (Picador, 2018)

Extracts from 'Maternal Landscapes' by Carolina Alvarado Molk in *The Best, Most Awful Job: Twenty Writers Talk Honestly About Motherhood*, edited by Katherine May (Elliott & Thompson, 2020)

'The Red Wheelbarrow' by William Carlos Williams, edited by Walton Litz and Christopher MacGowan; *Collected Poems Volume I 1909–1939*, reprinted by kind permission of Carcanet Press, Manchester, UK.

By William Carlos Williams, from THE COLLECTED POEMS: VOLUME I, 1909–1939, copyright © 1938 by New Directions Publishing Corp. Reprinted by permission of New Directions Publishing Corp.

Mad, Bad, and Sad: A History of Women and the Mind Doctors from 1800 to the Present by Lisa Appignanesi (Little, Brown

Book Group, 2009). Reproduced with the permission of the Licensor through PLSclear.

Extracts from *The Empathy Exams* by Leslie Jamison (Granta Books, 2015)

Extract from *A Life's Work* by Rachel Cusk (Faber & Faber, 2001)

Extracts from *Little Labours* by Rivka Galchen (Fourth Estate, 2017)

Extract from *High Fidelity* by Nick Hornby (Penguin, 1995)

Extracts from *Camera Lucida* by Roland Barthes (Vintage, 1993)

Extracts from *The Body Keeps the Score: Mind, Brain and the Body in the Transformation of Trauma* by Bessel van der Kolk (Penguin, 2015)

Extracts from *Book of Mutter* by Kate Zambreno (Semiotexte, 2017)

Extracts from *The Argonauts* by Maggie Nelson (Graywolf Press, 2016)

Extract from *With Child: A diary of motherhood* by Phyllis Chesler (Chicago Review Press, 2018)